OUTDOOR

ENTERTAINING

OUTDOOR

PICNICS, PARTIES, AND PORTABLE FEASTS

ENTERTAINING

ELIZABETH SAHATJIAN

PHOTOGRAPHS BY
RICHARD JEFFERY

INTRODUCTION BY
MARTHA STEWART

ARTABRAS PUBLISHERS NEW YORK

Originally published as *Outdoor Pleasures*
Published by arrangement with Stewart, Tabori & Chang, Inc.
Artabras edition 1991

Library of Congress Cataloging-in-Publication Data

Sahatjian, Elizabeth.
   [Outdoor pleasures]
   Outdoor entertaining : picnics, parties, and portable feasts / Elizabeth Sahatjian ; photographs by Richard Jeffery ; introduction by Martha Stewart.—1st Artabras ed.
      p.   cm.
   Originally published: Outdoor pleasures. New York : Stewart, Tabori & Chang : Distributed by Workman Pub., c1985.
   Includes index.
   ISBN 0-89660-017-3
   1. Outdoor cookery.   2. Entertaining.   3. Picknicking.
I. Jeffery, Richard.   II. Title.
TX823.S22   1991   642'.3—dc20   90-46854
                                                   CIP

The recipes included in *Outdoor Entertaining* appear through the courtesy of the following:

Dorothy Brummel: pages 58–63
Patrick R. Donahue, Rory's Inc.: pages 147–49, top
Sara Foster: pages 160–64; 202, top; 203
Marsha Harris: pages 178, bottom; 183, bottom
Ibi Hinrichs: page 177, bottom
Gay Jordan, Inc., Bespoke Food: pages 98–107
Carol McDonnell and Margit Corby: pages 142–46
Zarela Martinez: pages 132–35
Jean-Claude Nédélec, Chef and Co-Owner, Glorious Food, Inc.: pages 190–95; 218–22
Bradley Ogden, Chef, and Steven Fromer, Pastry Chef, Campton Place Hotel: pages 72–76
Dorian Leigh Parker: pages 206–7
Cynthia Pawlcyn: pages 234–35
Peter Kump's New York Cooking School: pages 84–88
Lynne and Wayne Rogers: pages 18–21
Wayne Rogers: pages 174; 183, top
Gary Sheldon: page 114, top
Jane Stacey: pages 172; 175; 176; 177, top; 181; 202, bottom; 208
Carol Steele and Kim Howard of C. Steele and Co.: pages 28–31
Martha Stewart with Donna Scott: pages 40–47
Susan Ward: pages 149, bottom; 150

Recipe editing: Stephanie Curtis
Design: J.C. Suarès, Kathleen Gates

Printed in Hong Kong.

INTRODUCTION

We are a nation of backyards, balconies, patios, beach houses, boats, parks, and endless miles of countryside accessible for picnics. More than people of any other country I have visited, we love to cook and entertain outdoors. Some of our oldest and strongest food traditions involve forms of outdoor cookery —the barbecue, the clambake, and the campfire—and we have added to our outdoor repertoire by adapting techniques and foods from the English, Italian, French, and Mexican cuisines. In creating the special picnics, parties, and portable feasts for this book—and for the *New York Times* "Entertaining" section that inspired it—photographer Richard Jeffery, author Elizabeth Sahatjian, and I worked closely with great cooks, both famous and unknown; all of these cooks had a vision about the ideal outdoor entertainment, which combined their favorite foods with their favorite environment.

One of the best examples is Paul Prudhomme, the brilliant chef-owner of K-Paul's in New Orleans, whose favorite place for outdoor cooking is the Atchafalaya Swamp where he prepared two of his favorite dishes, a huge smothered beef and a crawfish gumbo.

I had traveled to Bayou country with Richard Jeffery and a small crew of assistants to work with Paul on this outdoor event for the *New York Times*. At 4 A.M. we met Paul and his burly young chefs for the adventurous drive to the swamplands. After stopping three times—once for a breakfast of sugar-coated beignets, once for freshly made boudin blanc (a kind of Cajun blood sausage) and ice-cold Dixie beer, and finally for ten pounds of live crawfish for the gumbo—we ar-

Martha Stewart's homemade smokehouse is put to good use. Shown here are smoked oysters, shrimp, lobsters, poultry, and beef.

Paul Prudhomme stirs his roux, which cooks in a cast iron skillet over a powerful propane flame.

Ed Giobbi's barbecued baby lamb, ready for carving. Giobbi makes an accompanying mint pesto sauce using equal parts of mint and basil.

rived at our picnic destination, a verdant knoll surrounded by murky water on all sides.

In no time the propane stoves were lit and Paul was cooking—on one burner the smothered beef, on the other, roux for the gumbo. We talked, photographed, and drank beer while the delicious aromas wafted through the air. Finally we and the entire crew savored the results of Paul's outdoor Cajun kitchen.

Another great outdoor cook, with a very different style but equal dedication to his art, is Ed Giobbi. Ed enjoys entertaining in the yard of his Westchester home, where he gardens, raises grapes for his own wine, and paints. While Paul Prudhomme's style of cooking can be found only in America, Ed's is an interpretation of the great Italian culinary tradition.

On the particular day that we joined Ed, he had dug a shallow trench and constructed a simple rotisserie on which he would roast a whole baby lamb. The lamb was rubbed inside and out with olive oil and stuffed with large branches of fragrant rosemary and long sprigs of mint. Dressed and seasoned, the lamb weighed sixty pounds and was cooked to perfection in approximately six hours.

To accompany the lamb, Ed prepared a large bowlful of his special pesto, made from fresh basil and mint, both hand chopped. The meal of cold pasta, lamb, mint pesto, and garden salad was served at Ed's homemade wooden table on plates he and his family had designed and painted. It was delicious.

My own favorite location for outdoor entertaining is the backyard flower gardens of our home in Westport, Connecticut. My family and I are always designing and building areas around our house that can be used for entertaining

our friends. Often a dinner will center around our smokehouse, where an entire menu can be prepared. The pumpkin patch is a favorite setting for a quiet luncheon; and our stone terrace, shaded by a sycamore maple tree, is furnished with old-fashioned outdoor dining tables and chairs for tea parties, dinner parties, or cocktail gatherings.

Outdoor entertaining is particularly inviting, and because it is more informal, it is easier and somehow more fun. It brings together the places we love, the food we enjoy preparing, and the friends we want to see. It connects intimately the seasons and the foods of the season. Above all, outdoor entertaining is pleasurable.

I would like to thank the following people for their time and talents in helping to make this beautiful book: Carrie Donovan and Alison McFarland of the *New York Times*; Necy Fernandes, Sara Foster, Lisa Krieger, Dana Munro, Wendye Pardue, Dorian Leigh Parker, Donna Scott, Jane Stacey, Carol Steele, and Sudie Woodson for styling; and all my friends whose homes and grounds we photographed.

Martha Stewart

Chef Prudhomme's feast: a cast iron casserole filled with smothered beef and a large kettle of crawfish gumbo.

C L A M M I N G   I T   U P

NEW ENGLAND
CLAMBAKE

Skewered Shrimp and Scallops

Grilled Clams with Barbecue Sauce

Stuffed Cabbage Leaves

Roasted Leeks

Roasted Peppers

Grilled Sea Bass

Grilled Bluefish

Grilled Trout

Seafood-Stuffed Corn Husks

Summer is the most benignly obtrusive of seasons, when that persistent factor, heat, influences our moods and determines our actions, when we live and play mainly out-of-doors, as if we have just taken a two-month lease on July and August and must grasp every available moment of warm-weather pleasure. Appropriately, this is also a time of frequent entertaining, of open-air parties that go on for hours as families and friends share good, simple food and relaxation. And when the gathering spot is a stretch of beach, one of the most glorious modes of entertaining is the traditional clambake, an opportunity to share the abundance of land and sea.

This seasonal feast originated in New England with the Algonquin Indians, who would first gather a large variety of shellfish and fish from nearby waters, including lobsters, oysters, tiny bay scallops, littleneck clams, and large pieces of halibut. The seafood was placed over a bed of heated rocks in an open pit at the beach, then covered with a blanket of seaweed and steamed. It was a simple cooking technique and an excellent method of preserving the individual character of the foods while also allowing the flavors to blend with each other in the smoky, aromatic pit.

The contemporary appeal of this custom is obvious: the finest of fresh ingredients, foods cooked in a light manner that accentuates natural flavors, a feeling of union between participants and the environment. And as recent interest in our American culinary heritage attests, the foods and recipes of the past are a wonderful resource for the present-day cook and host.

Adapting a good idea to suit a personal style is the special forte of Wayne and Lynne Rogers of Westport, Connecticut. Inveterate cookbook collectors, worldwide travelers, and lovers of good food and drink, the Rogers' are frequent hosts to a familiar group of guests who have come to expect "something wonderful and sensationally clever whenever we're lucky enough to be invited," as one friend remarked. The Rogers' have defined their approach to food with impeccably fine ingredients, meticulous attention to detail, and natural presentation that is combined with a near-scholarly zeal for researching and developing unusual culinary techniques. They are continually experimenting with methods and new foods and refining recipes until they are deemed suitable to serve at their frequent events.

One such gathering took place on a hot day in mid-August. Thirty friends have been invited to the Rogers' for swimming and dining at their beachside home. For the occasion, Lynne and Wayne prepare a clambake that would do an Algonquin chief proud. Preparations for the event began well in advance with a trip to the lumberyard. Wayne had the idea

Skewers of shrimp and scallops, herb-wrapped trout and bluefish, and stuffed corn husks and clams.

Star attraction of the event—the eponymous clam.

of using a series of stackable wooden boxes to hold the food during the cooking. Using two-by-fours, he constructed several two-foot square boxes with wire meshing stapled to the bottom of each. Since they were all the same size, the boxes could be stacked, those with faster-cooking foods placed on top of the pile so the steam from the bottom layers would filter up gradually to those above. Unlike the traditional deep pit and seaweed clambake, Wayne's plan was to build a shallow trench, one foot deep, six feet across, and two feet wide, and fill it with charcoal and wood. After the fire is lit and blazing, the coals are allowed to calm to a gray ash and the boxes of seafood placed on top to cook.

For this updated clambake, Lynne has prepared a variety of fresh fish and vegetables that offer unusual blendings of color, texture, and flavor. Everything has been assembled in advance and each box has been filled with items that will cook at the same time. To retain the foods' natural juices, Lynne uses vegetable wrappers such as corn husks and cabbage leaves to form neat bundles of tiny bay scallops, shrimp, and fresh herbs. This is a large party so the Rogers use several boxes for these items; for smaller parties, a single box would suffice for all foods that require similar cooking times.

Using more than one cooking method enhances the appeal of the Rogers' clambake; their wooden boxes are also used to hold skewers of vegetables and whole fish as they are grilled over the hot coals. Bluefish, trout, and sea bass are particularly good prepared in this manner, after being wrapped with fresh herbs such as basil and oregano. Yellow and red peppers and tender leeks are also grilled while the seafood cooks. Big bowls of salad greens including arugula, radicchio, dandelion greens, and fresh basil and mint in a light vinaigrette add a colorful, crisp accent to the menu.

As clambakes are help-yourself occasions, Lynne favors understated service pieces and decorations—simple oversize dinner plates for the generous portions of food, balloon wine goblets, bunches of dahlias, daisies, and marigolds loosely arranged in pottery vases. If the party takes place away from home, Lynne advises packing baskets or attractive hampers of cutlery and tableware, which will serve as carrying containers and

On a hefty wooden slab, rhubarb and apple tarts, juicy-sweet and flaky, are ready for dessert.

also as receptacles handsome enough to place on the buffet.

It takes a long while from lighting the first pieces of kindling to the close of the meal, so dessert should be a bit audacious, yet uncomplicated. For their party, Wayne has made large, free-form fruit tarts filled with thick slices of apple or tangy rhubarb and nothing more than a sprinkling of sugar.

Hours later, a last ribbon of smoke from the fire spirals into the air, dances a solo jig, then vanishes. Tumblers of iced tea are replenished. There's talk of a quick volleyball game even though twilight is gradually giving way to darkness. And still, no one wants to head home.

Lynne used metal skewers for the sea scallops and unpeeled shrimp and pure cotton string to tie the herbs around the fish and to secure the cabbage packets.

SKEWERED SHRIMP AND SCALLOPS

½   pound sea scallops
    Fresh basil leaves
½   pound large shrimp, peeled (tails left on)
      and deveined
    Scallion tops (about 3 inches long)
½   cup butter, melted
¾   cup beer
    Salt
    Freshly ground black pepper

Wrap a scallop in a basil leaf and thread onto a 6-inch skewer. Wrap a shrimp with a scallion top and add to the skewer. Follow with another basil-wrapped scallop and a scallion-top-wrapped shrimp and a third basil-scallop. Prepare remaining scallops and shrimp in this manner and thread onto remaining skewers.

Combine butter and beer and brush generously over skewers. Sprinkle with salt and pepper. Lay skewers on a grill about 3 inches from hot coals and grill for about 5 minutes on each side, or until fish is just cooked through: Do not overcook, as scallops will become leathery.

Makes 6 to 8 servings

GRILLED CLAMS WITH BARBECUE SAUCE

2 dozen littleneck clams in the shell, scrubbed
½ cup barbecue sauce (recipe follows)

Place clams on a grill as close as possible to extremely hot coals and grill until they open, about 10 minutes.

Leaving clams on grill, remove the top half of each shell with the point of a sharp knife. Dab about 1 teaspoon of sauce on each clam. Serve immediately.

Makes 4 appetizer servings

Barbecue Sauce

3 tablespoons olive oil
1 medium-size onion, minced
3 cloves garlic, minced
1 6-ounce can tomato paste
½ cup red or white wine
¼ cup cider vinegar
 Juice of 1 lemon
¼ cup honey
¼ cup Worcestershire sauce
2 tablespoons Dijon-style mustard
1 tablespoon Tabasco (or to taste)
1 bay leaf
 Salt
 Freshly ground black pepper

Heat olive oil in saucepan over medium heat, and sauté onion and garlic until translucent but not browned. Add remaining ingredients, stir well, and simmer for 20 minutes.

Makes about 1 cup sauce

STUFFED CABBAGE LEAVES

10 to 12 large unblemished cabbage leaves
1½ pounds fresh medium shrimp, peeled and deveined
1½ pounds bay or sea scallops
1 cup butter, melted
½ cup sweet vermouth
1 tablespoon fresh thyme, or 1 teaspoon dried
¼ cup chopped fresh basil leaves or parsley
 Salt
 Freshly ground black pepper
 Scallion tops

Blanch cabbage leaves in a large pot of boiling salted water until crisp-tender, 3 to 5 minutes.

Plunge them into cold water, drain and pat dry. Lay leaves out flat and cut a wedge from the core end of each leaf to remove hard spine.

Pile a handful of shrimp and scallops into the center of each cabbage leaf. Brush with melted butter and vermouth, sprinkle with thyme and basil, and season with salt and pepper. Fold in the sides of each leaf, then roll up to make a tight package and tie each with a scallion top or string.

Place stuffed leaves on a grill about 2 to 3 inches from hot coals and cook for 5 to 7 minutes on each side.

Makes 10 servings

ROASTED LEEKS

8 large leeks
Dry white wine
½ cup olive oil
Salt
Freshly ground black pepper

Trim and discard the roots and dark green portions of the leeks, rinse thoroughly, and soak in cold water for 30 minutes to remove all sand and grit. Drain and pat dry. Place leeks on a wire rack in a roasting pan and add wine (or water) to a depth of about 1 inch, or to just below the level of the rack. Cover the pan tightly and steam over medium-low heat until leeks are softened, about 5 minutes.

Remove leeks from the roasting pan, brush generously with the oil, and season with salt and pepper. Place on a grill 2 to 3 inches from hot coals and grill, turning frequently, until slightly blackened all over, 6 to 10 minutes in all.

Makes 4 servings

ROASTED PEPPERS

8 large yellow peppers
8 large red peppers
½ cup whole fresh basil leaves, plus 1½ cups chopped
½ cup olive oil
3 tablespoons red wine vinegar
2 cloves garlic, minced
Salt
Freshly ground black pepper

Place peppers on a grill as close as possible to very hot coals and grill, turning occasionally, until skins are completely blackened all around.

Place blackened peppers in a large paper bag, close tightly, and let them "sweat" for 10 to 15 minutes. Remove from the bag and rinse under cold running water, rubbing off charred skin with your fingers. Drain thoroughly on paper towels. Core and seed peppers and cut lengthwise into quarters. Place in a mixing bowl with basil, oil, vinegar, and garlic. Season with salt and pepper and toss well.

Makes 8 servings

GRILLED SEA BASS

1 whole 4- to 5-pound sea bass
1 lemon, thinly sliced
1 lime, thinly sliced
Salt
Freshly ground black pepper
1 bunch fresh basil
1 bunch fresh oregano
6 tablespoons olive oil or sweet butter, melted

Rinse the bass in cold water and pat dry. Place lemon and lime slices in the cavity of the fish and season with salt and pepper. Tie basil and oregano leaves and sprigs around the fish with sturdy kitchen string. Brush generously with olive oil or butter. Place the fish on a grill about 4 inches away from very hot coals and grill for 20 to 25 minutes on each side, until the fish flakes away from the bone. Be careful not to break fish when turning it.

Makes 8 to 10 servings

GRILLED BLUEFISH

1   whole 3- to 4-pound bluefish
1   lemon, thinly sliced
1   lime, thinly sliced
    Salt
    Freshly ground black pepper
1   large bunch lovage, celery leaves, dill, or
    fennel

Rinse the bluefish in cold water and pat dry.
Place lemon and lime slices in the cavity of the
fish and season with salt and pepper. Separate
lovage leaves and wrap and tie around bluefish.
Place on a hot grill about 4 inches away from
very hot coals and grill for 20 to 25 minutes on
each side, until the fish flakes away from the
bone. Be careful not to break fish when turning it.

Makes 6 to 8 servings

GRILLED TROUT

6   1½-pound whole trout, cleaned and scaled
    Salt
    Freshly ground black pepper
12 branches fresh sage
12 branches fresh fennel leaves
    Olive oil or melted butter for basting

Wipe the cavity of each trout and season with
salt and pepper. Lay a sage and fennel branch on
each side of each trout and tie with twine at two
or three points to hold in place. Brush each trout

*Roasted peppers tossed with olive oil, garlic, and fresh
basil are a zesty accompaniment for the seafood.*

with oil or butter.
   Place on a grill over hot coals and grill for 10
to 15 minutes on each side, until flesh is white
and firm.

Makes 6 servings

SEAFOOD-STUFFED CORN HUSKS

6   to 8 corn husks
1   pound shrimp
½   pound bay scallops
4   tablespoons lemon juice
6   scallions, chopped
    Salt
    Freshly ground black pepper

Remove corn from husks, being careful not to

tear. Fill the husks with shrimp and scallops and
sprinkle with lemon juice, scallions, salt, and
pepper. Bring husks back together, tie tops with
a piece of husk, and place on hot grill for 10 to
15 minutes, turning several times. Open one
husk after about 10 minutes to check doneness
of seafood.

Makes 6 to 8 servings

C A R E F R E E   L I V I N G

SOUTHWESTERN
PICNIC

Yellow Pepper Soup

Chili Corn Bread

Chicken Stuffed with Goat Cheese

Carol's Salsa

Grilled Skirt Steak

Grilled Vegetables

Pomegranate Seeds and Orange
Sections with Tequila

Early October's tempo is a curiosity, part slack, part acceleration. Although the morning sun still gleams with warming light, there is a new sting to the air. With miserlike intensity we begin to hoard and linger over those increasingly rare days when mild weather and blue skies beckon.

This mood lends a particular quality to outdoor entertainments presented during the fall. Menus become more elaborate and feature heartier foods in response to cooler temperatures. Likewise, table settings take on a richer and more fully developed style.

To the citizens of Carefree, Arizona, October arrives with the verve of an old-fashioned screen door, swinging open wide to the outdoors. After weeks of blistering 100-degree-in-the-shade temperatures, the heat is just breaking now to a mild 70 degrees, a signal for many local residents to leave their air-conditioned sanctuaries and go out to enjoy the surrounding countryside. Located 20 miles north of Phoenix, this small town of 1,700 people is nestled at the edge of the Tonto National Forest, a vast area of deserts, mountains, clear lakes, and meandering tributaries. Although Saturdays are usually hectic for Carol Steele, owner of C. Steele and Co., a charming cafe and bakery with branches in both Phoenix and Scottsdale, today is set aside for leisure. With her associate Kim Howard, Carol has planned an extensive southwestern outdoor picnic and invited friends and family to rendezvous at noon before setting out to an undisclosed picnic site.

As guests arrive they are greeted and directed to pick up one of the many picnic baskets laden with provisions for the outing. With everyone bearing a load, the job is easy, as Carol and Kim lead the way on a brisk half-mile walk to a clearing set within the pink sands and gently sloping dunes of the Sonoran Desert. Long familiar with the striking beauty of the surrounding landscape, Kim and her in-laws, Henry and Lenore Howard, carefully selected the site for its dramatic panorama of different cacti. First-time visitors linger to scrutinize the various species, including the palo verde, tall and lank as an ancient totem pole standing erect against the skies; bushes of ocotillo; the saguaro, unique to the Sonoran Desert; prickly pear; and mormon tea, the leaves of which are brewed as a home remedy for stomach ailments. Small brown cactus wrens are busily building a nest in a nearby cactus, and someone spots a Gambel's quail with its distinguishing topknot of gray and brown feathers.

At the picnic site Carol and Kim spread brightly striped Mexican serapes and washable Indian cotton bedspreads over the sand. The Howards are avid collectors of American Indian basketry and Mexican pottery, and for the occasion they have lent an array of

Heirloom American Indian baskets and terra cotta pottery accent the lavish menu.

heirloom serving pieces and accessories that enhance the setting with a characteristically southwestern style of elegance: earthy, warm, and flamboyant.

In choosing the menu Carol and Kim decided on a southwestern flavor, enlivened with their innovative flourishes and departures from traditional recipes. They planned to present a buffet featuring a variety of items made with fresh, local ingredients and seasonings that could all be barbecued in advance the morning of the event. A barbecue offers ease and simplicity, since vegetables, meats, and poultry can all be cooked on the grill, and the cook can have a complete meal prepared in a couple of hours.

According to Kim, the regional cooking of Arizona is a combination of local and Mexican influences. Graced by rich farmlands, the region produces an abundance of corn, squash, tomatoes, and other vegetable crops as well as citrus fruits including oranges, lemons, and Mexican limes. In addition, thousands of acres are devoted to chili peppers, including mild poblano chiles, fiery small jalapeños, and serrano chiles, which are used fresh, or dried to incendiary hotness on the vine. Typically, native cooks use fresh citrus to accent entrées, drinks, and desserts, and either fresh or dried chili peppers appear at every meal of the day, whether chopped into scrambled eggs for breakfast or sprinkled over cheese for a midnight snack of nachos. Green tomatoes and flour tortillas reflect the influence of northern Mexico where wheat is grown and used in place of the traditional corn in tortillas.

The buffet begins as the Howards offer thirsty guests a refreshing cooler of club soda, bitters, and lime served in handsome Mexican goblets. For the first course there is Yellow Pepper Soup, golden as a pool of sunlight and poured hot from thermoses into mugs, then garnished with tortilla strips, sour cream, and fresh cilantro. Its snappy flavor and silken texture prove an apt introduction to the feast that soon follows.

Entrées include meat and poultry, both grilled early the morning of the picnic over mesquite cactus that had been gathered from the nearby desert and chopped into kindling for the barbecue. Plump roasting chickens stuffed with a mixture of mild goat cheese, butter, and cilantro, and basted with lime butter during grilling, are ready to be carved. Nearby a large pottery serving dish holds slices of richly charred skirt steak that smells fragrantly of olive oil and garlic. It is served with red, yellow, and purple bell peppers, along with seared halves of white eggplant. Butternut squash, drizzled with maple syrup and orange juice, and ears of fresh corn grilled in their husks provide excellent accompaniments to both entrées. Guests help themselves to spoonfuls of Carol's special salsa, redolent with ripe tomatoes, scallions, and jalapeño peppers. Flour tortillas, chili-flecked cornbread, and whole-grain bread complete the appealing array of specialties, and, as in all well-planned picnics, there is food in abundance for repeat helpings.

A robust menu, simple to prepare yet interesting with its regional flavor and vivid colors, this picnic buffet is especially appropriate for autumn entertaining, when vegetables and fruits are bountiful. Cool weather stimulates appetites, and outdoor feasts should include substantial, hearty items with at least one warm food, such as the Yellow Pepper Soup, ready to be served immediately. Grilled foods are always welcome, and they are especially suitable for picnics, as their flavors are preserved even when served at room temperature. After grilling the food in advance, it can be arranged on serving platters and wrapped tightly with aluminum foil. Serving platters can be placed in large shallow baskets for easy transporting to the picnic site.

As the warmth of the afternoon fades with the passing sunlight, Carol and Kim pass trays of dessert—seeds of pomegranates mixed with orange segments then doused with a generous splash of tequila; the fruit is dazzling in color, like the rich pattern of an Incan mosaic, and tastes of honey and the sun. Miles away high in the desert sky, a lone hot-air balloon comes into view, cruising in and out of the clouds in a game of hide and seek. For a minute it seems to stop in mid air, hovering like a huge white moth with barely a movement, and then slowly fades away.

Handblown Mexican goblets filled with club soda, bitters, and lime juice, a favorite southwestern-style cocktail.

Yellow Pepper Soup is a smooth purée of sweet, golden peppers, onion, chicken stock, and a touch of garlic.

YELLOW PEPPER SOUP

2 tablespoons sweet butter
½ medium onion, finely chopped
1 rib celery, finely chopped
2 cloves garlic, minced
3 large yellow peppers, cored, seeded, and sliced
3 tablespoons red wine vinegar
½ teaspoon Tabasco
6 cups chicken stock
   Salt
   Freshly ground white pepper

TO SERVE:
   Sour cream
   Chopped fresh cilantro leaves
   Fried corn tortillas, cut in ½-inch strips

Melt the butter in a medium skillet, add onion, celery, and garlic and sauté over medium heat until softened but not browned, about 5 minutes. Add peppers and sauté 5 minutes longer. Remove from the heat and let cool briefly. Turn peppers into a food mill or processor and purée.

In a medium saucepan, combine vinegar, Tabasco, and chicken stock and bring to a boil. Stir in puréed pepper mixture, season with salt and pepper, and simmer over medium heat for a few minutes longer. Serve hot, garnished with sour cream, chopped cilantro, and tortilla strips.

Makes 6 to 8 servings

CHILI CORN BREAD

3 eggs, beaten
1 cup buttermilk
½ cup sweet butter, melted and cooled briefly
1 cup fresh sweet corn kernels
1 cup white corn meal
3 teaspoons baking powder
½ teaspoon salt
1 green poblano chili, roasted, peeled, and chopped, or 2 ounces canned chilies, drained
1½ cups grated Monterey Jack cheese

Preheat oven to 350 degrees.

In a medium mixing bowl, combine eggs, buttermilk, butter, and corn and blend well. Combine corn meal, baking powder, and salt in a large mixing bowl. Pour liquid gradually, but quickly, into corn meal, mixing just until dry ingredients are moistened; do not overmix. Turn batter into a greased 8-inch square cake pan. Sprinkle chilies and cheese over the top and bake in the center of the oven for 45 minutes, or until top is golden brown.

Makes 6 to 8 servings

CHICKEN STUFFED WITH GOAT CHEESE

4 ounces fresh, mild goat cheese, softened
2½ tablespoons sweet butter, softened
2 tablespoons chopped fresh cilantro leaves
Salt
Freshly ground black pepper
1 5-pound roasting chicken
1 cup lime butter (recipe follows)

Combine goat cheese, butter, and cilantro in a mixing bowl or food processor and blend or process until smooth and thoroughly mixed. Season with salt and pepper to taste.

Carefully loosen the skin over the breast of chicken with your fingers and stuff goat cheese mixture between skin and breast meat, patting the mixture out as evenly as possible. Pull skin back into place. Truss chicken. Brush generously with lime butter.

Place the chicken on a grill 4 to 6 inches from very hot mesquite coals and grill, basting with lime butter and turning chicken every ten minutes so that it browns and cooks evenly for about 45 minutes, or until the juices run clear when chicken is pierced with a fork.

Makes 6 to 8 servings

Pungent cilantro and goat cheese enhance a plump chicken grilled over a mesquite fire.

Lime Butter

2 cups sweet butter, softened
¼ cup dry white wine
¼ cup half-and-half
¼ cup fresh lime juice
2 tablespoons grated lime zest

Place butter, wine, half-and-half, lime juice, and grated zest in a blender or food processor and process until smooth and well blended. Brush over vegetables and chicken while grilling.

Makes 2½ cups

CAROL'S SALSA

4 large ripe tomatoes, peeled and chopped
½ cup thinly sliced scallions (white and tender green part)
½ fresh jalapeño chili, minced
1 4-ounce can chopped green chilies, drained
2 tablespoons fresh lime juice
2 tablespoons chopped fresh cilantro leaves
½ teaspoon salt

Combine tomatoes, scallions, fresh and canned chilies, lime juice, cilantro, and salt in a medium mixing bowl and mix together well. Let stand at room temperature for at least an hour before serving to allow flavors to blend.

Makes 2½ cups

GRILLED SKIRT STEAK

1 3-pound, 1½-inch thick skirt steak
2 cloves garlic, halved lengthwise
    Olive oil
    Salt
    Freshly ground black pepper

Rub steak liberally all over with cut side of garlic cloves. Brush with oil and season well with salt and pepper. Place steak on a grill 4 to 6 inches above very hot mesquite coals and grill to desired doneness—3 to 4 minutes on each side for medium rare. Slice steak diagonally into ¼-inch thick slices and serve hot.

Makes 6 to 8 servings

GRILLED VEGETABLES

1 cup lime butter (recipe on page 29)
8 ears sweet corn in the husks
2 butternut squash, cut into wedges and seeded
8 whole red, yellow, and/or purple peppers
8 miniature white or purple eggplant, halved lengthwise
½ cup maple syrup
½ cup orange juice

Brush lime butter generously over all vegetables. Place corn and squash on a grill about 4 to 6 inches from very hot mesquite coals and grill for 2 to 3 minutes. Add peppers and eggplant and continue grilling vegetables, turning and brushing with lime butter, until tender and evenly charred; about 8 to 10 minutes longer. Total cooking time for corn and squash is 10 to 15 minutes; for peppers and eggplant, 8 to 10 minutes.

Blend maple syrup and orange juice. Remove vegetables from the grill, drizzle orange juice mixture over squash wedges, and serve hot.

Makes 6 to 8 servings

Above: For dessert there is a sunburst of ruby-red pomegranate seeds and orange sections sprinkled with ice-cold tequila.

Opposite: Flour tortillas and salsa accompany tender slices of Grilled Skirt Steak, mixed peppers, and eggplant.

A   G E N T L E R   A G E

TEA PARTY

Asparagus Tea Sandwiches

Hard-Cooked Quail Eggs

Cucumber Hearts with Herbed Cheese

Currant Scones with Peach Butter

Goat Cheese with Cream and Lemon

Madeleines

Sugar Cookies

Sherry-Soaked Pound Cake

Poached Peaches

Every summer for the past few years, lace-trimmed, blue parchment invitations have been sent from Martha Stewart, cookbook author and caterer, to a group of close women friends, requesting their presence at a very special tea party. It takes place on the expansive lawn and in the gardens that surround her white, shingled Colonial home in Connecticut. The event is one of the season's most anticipated by guests, who don floor-sweeping white linen dresses and appear on a Sunday afternoon bedecked as proper Edwardian ladies.

"I wanted to have a summer party that was a bit different and, unlike the usual picnics and poolside affairs, offered a time to lounge and dream, away from the hectic lives we lead all week long," explains Martha. "I thought of all the pastimes we associate with another era—embroidering, painting with a box of watercolors, sipping tea from a china cup as fragile as an eggshell—and I realized I was planning a turn-of-the-century tea party."

It is early afternoon, shortly before friends arrive for this year's gathering, and Mother Nature (this is, after all, a ladies-only event) has contributed a periwinkle-blue sky and a light breeze. Adding to the spirit of the day is the fact that this will be a baby shower, feting three-month-old Monica, daughter of one of the guests and the newest member of the annual group. In keeping with the feeling of reminiscence, Martha has asked each guest to bring a nostalgic gift, such as a pretty pincushion, an old-fashioned pop-up children's book, a stocking doll, as a present for Monica.

With due respect to Lewis Carroll, legend has cast the Duchess of Bedford as the creator of the first tea parties in eighteenth-century England. Known in London society as a clever hostess and a rich fount of gossip, the Duchess held afternoon gatherings for her fashionable friends in the lazy hours after luncheon and before the late evening supper. Small silver trays of delicate savories and cups of black tea poured from elegant porcelain tea services were served in her private drawing room, where many a social reputation was shattered.

Today's tea party, no less intimate but considerably more benevolent in intent, is held in the more natural setting of the outdoors. To protect food items from the late-June heat, Martha has placed a garden table in the shade of a sycamore maple tree. A colorful Victorian chintz quilt covers the table, and a white drawnwork cloth makes a contrasting runner. On the table, a pressed-glass, footed compote holds a flamboyant bouquet of roses in hues from pale pink to deep rose. The flowers complement pink lusterware dessert plates and a nineteenth-century pink and white porcelain tea service. Glass and silver trays are used for serving.

Numerous other arrangements and bouquets appear throughout the scene: a silver

Artist and guest Nina Duran adds her own winsome beauty to a vista of irises, poppies, and wildflowers.

compote filled with lupine, foxgloves, poppies, peonies, and more roses adorns the garden stone wall; a casual display of wild flowers including sweet william, coxcombs, and bleeding hearts is strategically placed in a muted corner to add color. A small round table with an arrangement of white tree peonies and astilbe is used to receive the brightly wrapped gifts each guest has brought for Monica.

For the menu, Martha has selected a variety of sweet and savory finger foods that are easy to eat and have unusual textural and flavor combinations. Color and presentation were considerations in determining the menu; the pastel tints of fresh summer produce—light pink peaches and pale green English cucumbers, for example—echo the colors in the nearby garden, and all serving

sampling the menu.

Among the starting selections are frosty green cucumber slices cut in heart shapes and filled with a delicate salmon mousse, arranged on a peony-adorned platter. Nearby on a silver tray, lightly blanched asparagus spears garnish savory tea sandwiches. Some tiny hard-cooked quail eggs are nestled amid fresh thyme in a silver basket; they are served with tangy seasoned salt. The centerpiece for the buffet is a log of Montrachet cheese in a white pool of lemon-flavored crème fraîche and decorated with ribbons of fresh chive and its purple blossoms—a creamy accompaniment to warm, flaky currant scones or herb biscuits.

Sweets include both traditional English tea party pastries as well as seasonal fruits gently poached or made into preserves. Old-fashioned sugar cookies cut into ovals or fluted rounds are everyone's favorite with iced mint or hot black pekoe tea. Tiny spongy-soft madeleines are good with the rose-hued peaches poached in red wine and peach brandy. A classic Edwardian sweet, sherry-soaked pound cake, has a tender, crumb-like texture and intense, winy flavor.

Sitting on lawn chairs after dining, four friends enjoy the stillness of a Sunday afternoon, the perfect June weather, and the pleasure of simply relaxing. At the small table Monica's mother is unwrapping presents. The

Even flower arrangements for the party contribute to the turn-of-the-century mood.

trays are garnished with flowers. To preserve freshness as well as the dainty aspect of the buffet table, Martha planned to put out small amounts of food and refill the trays with fresh selections when necessary. Since all items were prepared in advance and refrigerated or stored for last-minute serving, Martha is free to mingle with her friends as she invites everyone to help themselves to plates and begin

Huge white peony blossoms and white astilbe accent the birthday table laden with presents for Baby Monica.

large box with the pink satin ribbon contains a lovely hand-smocked baby dress, and she holds it up high for everyone to admire. In the garden a few yards away, a more ambitious friend is painting a still life of irises and poppies. Martha produces an old embroidery set she had found in the attic and someone remembers the lessons of her grandmother, including how to hold the needle properly and how not to pull the thread too tightly. Off in a shaded corner the baby is asleep in her pram. And if the Mad Hatter and a certain white rabbit had suddenly dropped by for a bite of scone, no one would have been surprised.

A pastel array of finger foods on old silver and pressed glass serving pieces.

ASPARAGUS TEA SANDWICHES

1 tablespoon fresh tarragon
1 teaspoon fresh lemon juice
1 cup mayonnaise, preferably homemade
1 tablespoon Dijon-style mustard
¼ teaspoon sugar
  Salt
  Freshly ground white pepper
10 extra-thin slices white bread, or homemade pain de mie
40 thin asparagus tips, blanched
1 medium ripe tomato, seeded and very
  thinly sliced

In a small bowl, soak the tarragon in the lemon juice. Drain off and discard lemon juice. Chop the tarragon. Combine tarragon, mayonnaise, mustard, and sugar in a small mixing bowl, season with salt and pepper and blend well.

Using a serrated knife, trim crusts from bread, stack in short stacks and cut through the center, then cut again, to make 40 uniform bread squares. Cover bread with a sheet of plastic wrap while preparing sandwiches to prevent it from drying out.

Spread each bread square lightly with tarragon mayonnaise. Top each with an asparagus tip and a tomato slice. Serve immediately, or cover with plastic wrap and refrigerate until ready to serve.

Makes 40 squares

HARD-COOKED QUAIL EGGS

24 quail eggs, at room temperature

SEASONED SALT:
½ cup coarse salt
1 teaspoon coarsely ground white pepper
  Pinch cayenne pepper
  Pinch paprika

Place eggs in a large, heavy saucepan. Add enough cold water to cover and bring to a boil over medium heat. Boil gently for 4 to 5 minutes.

Pour off hot water, fill saucepan with cold water to cover eggs and allow them to cool completely. Refrigerate until ready to use.

In a small bowl, combine salt, white and cayenne peppers, and paprika and store in a covered container until ready to use.

Peel eggs just before serving and serve with a dish of the seasoned salt to dip them in.

Makes 8 to 12 appetizer servings

Hearts and flowers: in this case the hearts are made of cucumber slices topped with creamy salmon mousse and, for decoration, a snip of peony.

CUCUMBER HEARTS WITH HERBED CHEESE

1   3-ounce package cream cheese, softened
1   tablespoon heavy cream or crème fraîche
     (see appendix)
1   tablespoon finely chopped fresh oregano,
     chervil, or basil leaves
1   tablespoon finely chopped scallions
1   tablespoon finely chopped parsley
     Salt
     Freshly ground black pepper
1   long, seedless cucumber

TO SERVE:
     Fresh oregano, chervil, or basil leaves

In a small mixing bowl, combine cream cheese, heavy cream, oregano, scallions, and parsley and blend together until smooth. Season to taste with salt and pepper and stir.

Slice cucumber into ¼-inch thick rounds and arrange on a flat work surface. Cut into heart shapes, using a small heart biscuit or cookie cutter slightly smaller in diameter than cucumber slices. (See note.)

Spoon the herbed cream cheese into a pastry bag fitted with a decorative tip and pipe mixture onto each cucumber heart. Garnish each with an oregano or basil leaf, or a sprig of chervil.

Makes 10 to 12 appetizer servings

Note: Heart-shaped cookie or biscuit cutters can be found in sets at gourmet cookware stores.

CURRANT SCONES WITH PEACH BUTTER

3 tablespoons brandy
1 cup currants
1 teaspoon grated orange zest
4½ cups flour
2 teaspoons baking powder
½ teaspoon baking soda
2 tablespoons sugar
1 cup sweet butter, cut into small pieces
1 cup heavy cream (approximately)

GLAZE:
1 beaten egg
¼ cup heavy cream

Place brandy, currants, and orange zest in a small bowl and allow to soak while preparing batter.

Combine flour, baking powder, baking soda, and sugar in a large mixing bowl. Add butter pieces and cut into flour with a fork or pastry blender until mixture resembles coarse meal. Mixing gently with your fingers, add just enough cream to make dough hold together. Add plumped currants and any liquid and work them into the dough. Form into a ball, wrap in plastic wrap and chill for at least 30 minutes.

(If using a food processor, combine butter with half of the dry ingredients and process with on/off motion until mixture resembles coarse meal. Add remaining dry ingredients and process briefly with on/off motion. Transfer dough to a mixing bowl and stir in enough cream to make it stick together. Mix plumped currants into dough, form into a ball, wrap, and chill for at least 30 minutes.)

Preheat oven to 375 degrees.

On a lightly floured surface, roll dough out to ½-inch thick for small scones (1-inch diameter) and ¾-inch thick for larger scones. Using biscuit or cookie cutters of different shapes, cut out dough and place scones on well-buttered or parchment-covered baking sheets. Blend together egg and cream and brush over tops of scones. Bake in the center of the oven for 13 to 15 minutes, until golden brown and puffed. Serve hot with peach butter (recipe follows).

Makes about forty 1-inch scones

Peach Butter

6 large, ripe peaches, peeled, pitted, and chopped
1 cup sugar
1 teaspoon ground cinnamon
½ teaspoon freshly grated nutmeg
  Pinch ground cloves
2 cups sweet butter, softened

In a medium saucepan, combine peaches, sugar, cinnamon, nutmeg, and cloves. If peaches are not very juicy, add a little water; up to 3 tablespoons. Simmer over medium heat for about 25 minutes, until fruit is soft and mixture is thick and syrupy. If mixture seems runny, increase heat and boil briefly to evaporate excess liquid. Remove from heat and let cool.

Place mixture in a food processor or electric blender and purée until smooth. In a medium mixing bowl, cream butter with a whisk until light and fluffy. Gently fold peach purée into butter. Add additional sugar if necessary, blend well and refrigerate until ready to use.

Makes 2 cups

Goat Cheese with Cream and Lemon: a snowy log of Montrachet napped with heavy cream and garnished with fresh chive blossoms and stems.

GOAT CHEESE WITH CREAM AND LEMON

1   cup heavy cream
1   tablespoon fresh lemon juice
½   teaspoon grated lemon zest
⅛   teaspoon sugar
    Pinch cayenne pepper
    Salt
2   10-ounce logs (about 1½ inches in diameter) goat cheese (such as Montrachet)

TO SERVE:
    Long chives with blossoms

In a small bowl, combine cream, lemon juice and zest, sugar, and cayenne. Season to taste with salt.

Place goat cheese logs side-by-side in a shallow dish just large enough to hold them. Pour cream mixture over cheese, cover with plastic wrap, and let marinate in the refrigerator for at least 2 or 3 hours.

Remove cheese from the refrigerator long enough before serving to allow it to warm to room temperature. Arrange chive stems and blossoms decoratively on top of each cheese log and serve surrounded by herb biscuits.

Makes about 12 appetizer servings

MADELEINES

4 eggs
¼ teaspoon salt
⅔ cup sugar
1 teaspoon vanilla
1 cup flour
½ cup sweet butter, melted and cooled

TO SERVE:
  Powdered sugar

Preheat oven to 375 degrees.

In a large mixing bowl, whisk the eggs, salt, sugar, and vanilla together until thick and pale yellow in color, about 8 minutes. Fold in flour, rapidly but gently. Gradually fold in butter, making sure it does not settle to the bottom of the bowl. (See note.)

Spoon batter into well-buttered, lightly floured madeleine tins, filling each about three-fourths full. Place in the center of the oven and bake until golden brown, about 10 minutes. Turn madeleines out of tins immediately and let cool on a rack. Before serving, dust lightly with powdered sugar.

Makes 3 dozen 3-inch madeleines

Note: The batter can be made entirely in electric mixer, using wire whip attachment.

SUGAR COOKIES

1 cup sweet butter, softened
2 cups sugar, plus additional for sprinkling over cookies
2 eggs
½ teaspoon vanilla extract
1 tablespoon brandy
4½ cups flour
4 teaspoons baking powder
1 teaspoon salt
½ cup milk

In a large mixing bowl, cream butter and sugar together with a whisk until light and fluffy. Add eggs, vanilla, and brandy and blend thoroughly.

Combine flour, baking powder, and salt. Add flour mixture to creamed butter 1 cup at a time, alternating with milk, and beating thoroughly after each addition. Divide dough into four parts, form into balls, wrap each in plastic wrap, and chill for at least 1 hour.

Preheat oven to 375 degrees.

On a lightly floured surface, roll out dough,

Buttery Sugar Cookies are as necessary as lemon on a proper tea table.

one ball at a time, to ⅛-inch thick and cut out with a 2- to 3-inch diameter cookie cutter. Place on buttered or parchment covered baking sheets and sprinkle each cookie lightly with sugar. Bake in the center of the oven for 8 to 10 minutes; do not allow cookies to brown. Transfer to wire racks and let cool.

Makes about forty 2- to 3-inch cookies.

Columbine blossoms decorate the tray of soft Madeleines.

For a traditional English touch: Sherry-Soaked Pound Cake, rich, dense, and flavorful.

SHERRY-SOAKED POUND CAKE

¾ cup sweet butter, softened
3 large eggs
1 cup sugar
   Grated zest of 1 lemon
1¼ cups sifted cake flour

TO FINISH:
½ cup sweet sherry
1 tablespoon sugar

Preheat oven to 350 degrees.

In a small mixing bowl, cream softened butter with a whisk until it reaches the consistency of a heavy, thick mayonnaise. Place bowl over a bowl of ice water to prevent it from softening further and set aside.

In an electric mixer, combine eggs, sugar, and lemon zest and blend at high speed for 5 to 6 minutes, or until mixture is pale and fluffy and has doubled in volume. Reduce mixer speed to low and sprinkle in flour gradually but rapidly (it should take no more than 20 to 30 seconds) so that egg mixture does not deflate. Continuing to mix at low speed, add whipped butter quickly, and blend for about 20 seconds only. (Butter will not be thoroughly incorporated at this point.) Turn off mixer and fold batter gently with a wooden spoon 2 or 3 times to finish incorporating butter.

Turn batter into a well-buttered and lightly floured 8-inch bundt or tube pan, or a kugelhopf mold. Tap pan lightly against a hard surface to remove air bubbles.

Place in the center of oven and bake for about 40 minutes, or until top is nicely browned and cake springs back when pressed lightly. Let cool in the pan for 10 minutes before turning cake out onto a wire rack to cool completely.

Pour sherry and remaining tablespoon sugar in the bottom of a rimmed, round cake platter just large enough to hold cake, and stir until sugar dissolves. Place cooled cake on platter on top of sherry, cover with aluminum foil and allow to soak up sherry overnight.

Makes 10 to 12 servings

Note: This cake can be made 2 days ahead and stored covered in the refrigerator until ready to serve.

POACHED PEACHES

SYRUP:
- **3** cups red wine
- **2** cups brandy
- **½** cup granulated sugar
- **½** cup firmly packed light brown sugar
  Zest of 2 lemons, cut into julienne strips

TO POACH:
- **1½** to 2 cups granulated sugar
  Zest of 1 lemon, cut into wide strips
- **1** cinnamon stick
- **10** large, ripe but firm peaches, unpeeled

TO SERVE:
- **10** mint leaves
- **10** 3-inch cinnamon sticks

In a large saucepan, combine red wine, brandy, granulated and brown sugars, and lemon zest. Bring to a boil and boil over medium-high heat until mixture has reduced to 3 cups and is very thick. Remove from the heat and refrigerate until cold.

Meanwhile, place 4 cups water, sugar, lemon zest, and cinnamon stick in a large stainless steel pot or Dutch oven and bring to a boil. Place peaches, stem-ends up, in pot and reduce heat. (If necessary, poach in two batches.) Add additional water, if necessary, to completely cover peaches. Bring to a slow simmer and cook over medium heat for about 3 minutes. (Their flesh should be barely tender and still quite firm.) Gently lift peaches from poaching liquid, drain and let stand until cool enough to handle. Using a sharp knife, remove about half of the peel from each peach, leaving wide strips of peel for an attractive presentation.

Arrange peaches, stem-ends up, in a shallow serving dish. Pour cooled syrup over and around peaches and garnish each with a mint leaf and a cinnamon stick.

Makes 10 servings

SKIPJACKS AND SHELLS

LUNCH ON THE CHESAPEAKE BAY

CRAB DIP

CRAB CAKES

FRENCH-FRIED OYSTERS

OYSTER FRITTERS

OYSTER STEW

OYSTER PIE

BLACK-EYED PEAS

CANDIED SWEET POTATOES

SPINACH SALAD

CORN MUFFINS

SWEET POTATO PIE

PECAN PIE

Within is a country that may have the prerogative over the most pleasant places knowne, for large and pleasant navigable Rivers, heaven and earth never agreed better to frame a place for man's habitation.... Here are mountaines, hils, plaines, valleyes, rivers, and brookes, all running most pleasantly into a faire Bay, compassed but for the mouth, with fruitfull and delightsome land.*

———

This was the Chesapeake Bay of over three hundred years ago that inspired Captain John Smith in his account of the maiden exploration of the area. Sailing northward past the capes of Charles and Henry, Smith and his crew had arrived at this uncharted region of innumerable coves and inlets, marshlands and sinuous waterways that extended from Virginia all the way to Maryland. What they discovered there was a paradise of natural abundance created by the intricate alliance of land and sea.

For nearly 4,000 miles, the Bay, as it is simply called, stretches in a network of land, islands, and countless tributaries including the major rivers of the Susquehanna, Potomac, James, and York, all saturated with plant and animal life. A major portion of the United States' supply of oysters, crabs, and clams are taken from these waters each year by commercial fishermen; and on a smaller scale, striped bass and herring attract sport fishermen.

The lure of the region holds firm on the inhabitants here—the fishermen who traverse its waters for its trove of shellfish, the women who work long hours in the crab processing plants, dexterously extracting the flesh from recalcitrant cartilage, and the children who learn to swim before they can walk. For them, it is a strenuous life that requires endurance, courage, physical and emotional stamina in order to survive, but more people remain here than leave.

The growth, harvesting, and processing of the native blue crab and American oyster comprise the backbone of the Bay's economy. For the crabbers, spring is the beginning of the cycle, when they go out to catch the soft-shell crabs, the males and females that have shed their winter carapace for this first moult of the season. Summer and autumn are peak seasons for the "sooks" and "jimmies," mature females and males with their hard, blue shells. During these fishing months the crabbers set out before dawn on their workboat —log canoe or bugeye—to start culling the crabpots for their catch. Then in winter the cycle ends and the crabs withdraw to unapproachable reaches to hibernate.

The pursuit of oysters follows a different rhythm that begins with an early harvest in mid-September and reaches a crescendo in December when hundreds of oystermen work in bone-chilling temperatures dredging or

*The General Historie of Virginia, New England and the Summer Isles by Captain John Smith, James Maclehose and Sons, Glasgow, 1907, vol. 1.

A bulging net of oysters is hauled on deck by a hydraulic winch.

tonging the shoals for the hardy mollusks.

On this autumn morning, warm breezes and mild weather impart a tranquil charm to the dockside scene in Saint Michael's, a town on the northern tip of Maryland's Eastern Shore and seat of historic Talbot County. Ed Farley, skipper of the Stanley Norman, a skipjack built in 1902, is moored at the pier as a party of twelve vacationers, who have hired the boat and Captain Farley's services for the day, climb aboard. The group has arranged for a day of sailing and picnicking, capped by a hunt for first-of-the-season oysters that will be prepared and eaten on board in true Chesapeake fashion, with the salt spray still dripping wet on the shell.

Sails billowed wide with the wind, the boat cuts through the waves as the captain steers a

Frosty glasses of Bourbon Sours: a toast to Maryland's bounty.

course a few miles from shore. Coppery glints from the mid-morning sun dapple the water and the skipjack slows to a stop. To the untrained eye, the site is indistinguishable from the surrounding waters, but the obliging crew of picnickers follows Farley's advice to be prepared as he releases a winch and gradually lowers a nylon net into the waves. Sure enough, this is a fertile oyster bed and the net is soon raised to spill its generous haul on deck. The vacationers are ready with knives to shuck several dozen for immediate consuming.

In a few moments, only empty shells remain, a signal for Captain Farley to bring on the crabs, which have been cooked in advance. Newspapers are spread on deck, knives and mallets handed out, and Farley hoists onto middeck a basket of "blues" steamed to scarlet perfection in a broth of hot and spicy seasonings. As traditional accompaniments to this version of the Eastern Shore Dinner, there are platters of cheddar cheese cubes, sweet pickles, cider vinegar for a dipping sauce, and for the novice, instruction on the proper way to eat a crab—a matter of considerable controversy. According to the captain, who can down a half dozen sooner than it takes most of us to pick our way warily through a couple of claws, the way to begin is to place the crab on its back. With the handle of a knife or a mallet smash the two main claws to remove them. Lift and tear away the center body flap, then pull off and discard the hard back shell. Using a knife, remove the hairy "whiskers" and the rubbery-textured lungs on either side. Next, split the crab in half and cut down through the flesh to reveal the several meat-filled body chambers, then carefully extract this flesh with the point of the knife. Crack the claws at the pincer end and remove the meat by gradually pulling away the pincers. The remaining small claws and feelers can be broken off by hand; there will be a lump of sweet meat on the end of each for nibbling on with the cold beer Farley has brought along for the party.

As the skipjack resumes its course for a leisurely sail on the Bay, past patches of marsh grass and orange-red buoys marking the location of crabpots, a celebration sponsored by the members of the Talbot County Historical Society is underway in town. They have invited guests and visitors to a munificent sea-

For the true afficionado nothing equals the pleasure of oysters on the half shell.

food buffet lunch set amid the gardens of an eighteenth-century manor house. Tall poplars rim the house and trace a sloping path down to the shoreline. Sheep graze in the adjoining pastures and flocks of mallard ducks complain noisily from nearby pens as the party assembles on the patio to toast the abundance of the harvest season. Lest anyone forget that the Eastern Shore is south of the Mason-Dixon Line, there are pitchers of Bourbon Sours, a good introduction to the southern hospitality that follows.

At the water's edge a mammoth steamer kettle set over hot coals is brimming with juicy oysters to be served simply in their shells with a squirt of lemon juice and melted butter at the start of the meal. Close by, the buffet table is ready, set with a blue linen tablecloth. Dor-

Lunch on deck is a pile of boiled blue crabs, sweet and spicy hot.

othy Brummel and her daughter Cynthia are professional caterers and local residents, and for this occasion they have prepared a feast of traditional Chesapeake specialties. The Brummel style of cooking, a judicious mix of tradition and innovation, is straightforward, employing seasonal ingredients from nearby waters and farms. "Give Dorothy a dozen oysters and she'll fix them in as many ways," mar-

vels an old friend. Today she has prepared oysters fried with a light crumb breading, puffy fritters, a flaky, crust-topped pie, and a rich stew. To make the eating easier, Dorothy serves her crab picked from the shell and shaped into all-lump-meat cakes, nutty, sweet, and tender. Black-Eyed Peas and Candied Sweet Potatoes are hearty accompaniments.

After lunch, Society members invite visi-

Dorothy Brummel and her daughter Cynthia invite guests to enjoy the feast they've prepared.

tors for a tour of the nearby Chesapeake Bay Maritime Museum, which contains an excellent collection of vintage fishing craft. Upon returning, guests help themselves to dark-roasted coffee and two classic Southern pies —sweet potato and buttery pecan—while they watch a formation of brilliantly plumed ducks soar across the slate gray sky of deep-ening afternoon, a sure sign that winter will arrive soon and all of a sudden, the way it usually does here. In the distance, the Stanley Norman sails gracefully into view as it heads for port. On the horizon, the bobbing white triangles of distant sailboats grow larger by the minute; it's just about time to lay anchor, all along the Bay.

Above: Blue crabs from the Chesapeake Bay.

To eat the crabs, first twist and pull off the two large claws (the remaining legs can also be pulled off and the small amount of meat on the end eaten). With a sharp knife, pry off the pointed flap or "apron" on the underside and, turning the crab over, break off the entire top shell. Discard the yellow liver and the spongy gray lungs. Break the crab in half and remove as much meat as possible. With a mallet, crack the claws at the pincer end and pull out the sweet meat in one piece.

Opposite: All the essentials for a crab feast—hot crabs, steamed in a small amount of water and beer and hot seasonings, icy cold beer, cubes of cheddar cheese, sweet pickles, cider vinegar, spicy salt, and a knife and mallet.

A basket of "blues," indispensable to a traditional Eastern Shore Dinner.

CRAB CAKES

2	pounds Maryland backfin crab meat
½	cup butter
¼	cup finely chopped onion
¼	cup finely chopped celery
¼	cup fresh bread crumbs
2	eggs
1	tablespoon Worcestershire sauce
1	tablespoon hot dry mustard
3	tablespoons mayonnaise
	Pinch cayenne pepper
1	tablespoon Old Bay seasoning
1	cup oil or butter for frying

Drain and carefully pick over crab meat to remove pieces of shell and cartilage.

Melt butter in a large skillet, add onion and celery, and sauté over medium heat until softened. Place mixture in a mixing bowl with the crab meat, bread crumbs, eggs, Worcestershire, mustard, mayonnaise, cayenne, and Old Bay seasoning and mix together gently with your hands. Form into patties and refrigerate for at least an hour before browning.

Heat oil or butter in a large skillet, add crab cakes, and sauté over medium-high heat until lightly browned on each side, about 3 minutes per side.

Makes 6 to 8 servings

CRAB DIP

1   pound Maryland backfin crab meat
3   8-ounce packages cream cheese, softened
2   tablespoons French's mustard
1   tablespoon Worcestershire sauce
1½ teaspoons garlic powder
2   tablespoons powdered sugar
½   cup mayonnaise
⅔   cup dry vermouth
    Cayenne pepper

Drain and carefully pick over crab meat to remove pieces of shell and cartilage.

In a large saucepan, combine cream cheese, mustard, Worcestershire, garlic powder, sugar, and mayonnaise and beat together with a wire whisk until well blended. Place saucepan over low heat or gently simmering water and stir in vermouth and crab meat. Season with cayenne and heat gently, stirring, until warmed through.

Pour into a fondue pot or chafing dish and serve warm, surrounded by crackers.

Makes 6 to 8 servings

FRENCH-FRIED OYSTERS

2   cups oil or solid shortening for frying
2   dozen large fresh oysters (about 1 quart), shucked, rinsed, and patted dry
3   eggs, beaten
2   cups seasoned bread crumbs

SAUCE:
3   ounces chili sauce
1   tablespoon grated fresh horseradish
    Dash cayenne pepper

Heat oil in a large skillet over medium heat until a fresh bread cube sizzles vigorously when dropped into it. Dip oysters, one at a time, into the beaten egg, roll in bread crumbs, and drop immediately into hot oil. Let brown 3 to 4 minutes on a side, until a deep golden brown. Do not fry more than about 6 oysters at a time or the oil will cool down. Remove browned oysters from the oil with a slotted spoon, place on a baking sheet lined with paper towels, and keep warm in a low oven while frying successive batches of oysters.

Blend together the chili sauce, horseradish, and cayenne and pour into a sauceboat. Serve oysters hot, accompanied by sauce.

Makes 6 to 8 servings

OYSTER FRITTERS

2   cups flour
1   tablespoon baking powder
1   teaspoon salt
½   teaspoon freshly ground black pepper
2   eggs, beaten
¾   cup milk
2   tablespoons vegetable oil
2   dozen large fresh oysters, drained, liquor reserved
    Vegetable oil for frying

In a small mixing bowl, combine flour, baking powder, salt, and pepper. Gradually add eggs and milk, alternating the two and mixing well after each addition. Stir in 2 tablespoons of the reserved oyster liquor and the 2 tablespoons oil. The batter should be very thick. Gently fold oysters into the batter.

Heat the oil in a heavy medium skillet over medium heat until a bread cube sizzles and turns golden brown when dropped into it.

Dip a large tablespoon into the hot fat, then dip oysters out of the batter one at a time, along with a small amount of the batter. Drop into the hot oil and fry until browned all over, about 2 to 3 minutes on a side. Do not fry more than about 6 oysters at a time or the oil will cool down. Remove browned oysters from the oil with a slotted spoon, place on a baking sheet lined with paper towels, and keep warm in a low oven while frying successive batches of fritters. Serve hot.

Makes 6 to 8 servings

Oyster Stew is redolent with cream and butter.

OYSTER STEW

½   cup butter
1   quart small fresh oysters, drained, liquor
      reserved
4   cups half-and-half

Salt
Freshly ground black pepper

TO SERVE:
    Finely chopped parsley

In a large skillet, melt butter, add oysters, and warm gently over medium-low heat for 2 to 3 minutes, or just until their edges start to curl.

Meanwhile, in a large saucepan, warm half-and-half over medium heat until just beginning to simmer; do not let it boil. Mix half-and-half and oyster liquor together and stir into skillet with oysters, then pour all of oyster mixture back into saucepan. Season with salt and pepper, stir, and ladle into a terrine or individual soup bowls. Garnish with chopped parsley and serve immediately.

Makes 6 to 8 servings

OYSTER PIE

2   recipes pâte brisée (see appendix)
4   tablespoons butter
¼   cup chopped celery
¼   cup chopped onion
2   cups crushed soda crackers
1   quart fresh oysters, drained and
      patted dry
¼   teaspoon salt
¼   teaspoon freshly ground black pepper
1   10¾-ounce can cream of celery soup
½   cup half-and-half

On a lightly floured surface, roll out two-thirds of pastry dough into a ⅛-inch thick by 11-inch round or square and press into a 9-inch pie pan or square baking dish. Prick bottom and sides of dough with a fork and refrigerate for at least 30 minutes.

Preheat oven to 350 degrees.

Melt butter in a medium skillet. Add celery and onion and sauté over medium heat until softened.

Sprinkle a layer of cracker crumbs over the bottom of chilled pastry shell. Top with a layer of oysters and season with salt and pepper. Continue to layer remaining cracker crumbs and oysters in this manner, finishing with a layer of crumbs. Combine soup and half-and-half. Pour soup over crackers, then spread sautéed celery and onion mixture over the top. Roll out remaining pastry dough to a ⅛-inch thick by 9-inch round or square and lay over the top of pie. Trim pastry and crimp edges to seal. Use a sharp knife to cut small slits in the top of pastry to allow steam to escape.

Place pie in the center of oven and bake for 30 to 40 minutes, until oysters are cooked and pastry is lightly browned.

Makes 6 to 8 servings

What's southern hospitality without Black-Eyed Peas and Spinach Salad?

BLACK-EYED PEAS

1   country ham bone
1   teaspoon cayenne pepper
1   teaspoon salt
1   small onion, chopped
¼   cup sugar
2   pounds dried black-eyed peas, soaked over-
        night in 3 quarts water and drained
¼   pound salt pork, cubed (see note)
4   tablespoons butter

TO SERVE:
    Chopped parsley

Place the ham bone in a large heavy kettle with 6 cups water, cayenne, salt, onion, and sugar and simmer over medium-high heat for 30 minutes, until meat is falling off ham bone.

Add soaked and drained peas and salt pork and simmer over medium-low heat for 30 to 45 minutes. Stir in the butter and sprinkle with chopped parsley. Serve hot alone, or with rice or in a soup.

Makes 6 to 8 servings

Note: If you're using a fatty ham bone the salt pork is not necessary.

CANDIED SWEET POTATOES

6	medium sweet potatoes, scrubbed
½	cup butter
¼	cup freshly squeezed orange juice
1½	cups firmly packed light brown sugar
½	cup granulated sugar
1	tablespoon grated orange zest
1	tablespoon ground nutmeg

Place sweet potatoes in a large pot of boiling water, cover, and boil over medium heat for 20 to 30 minutes, or until fork-tender.

Meanwhile, melt butter in a medium saucepan. Stir in orange juice, brown and granulated sugars, orange zest, and nutmeg and simmer over medium-low heat until sugars are dissolved, stirring frequently to prevent sauce from sticking. Spoon 2 tablespoons of cooking water from sweet potatoes into sauce, stir, bring sauce to a boil and simmer over medium heat for 5 minutes, until thickened.

Preheat oven to 350 degrees.

Drain sweet potatoes. Peel and cut in half. Place in an 8-by-12-inch rectangular baking dish and pour sauce over the top. Place in the center of the oven and bake for 30 minutes, or until slightly browned.

Makes 6 to 8 servings

Candied Sweet Potatoes are a golden temptation.

CORN MUFFINS

2	cups white corn meal
½	cup flour
2	tablespoons baking powder
1	teaspoon salt
3	tablespoons sugar
¼	cup oil
2	eggs, lightly beaten
¾	cup milk, at room temperature
	About 6 tablespoons butter

Preheat oven to 400 degrees.

Combine corn meal, flour, baking powder, salt, and sugar in a large mixing bowl. In a separate bowl, whisk oil, eggs, and milk together. Make a well in the center of dry ingredients, pour in combined liquids, and blend quickly with a fork just until dry ingredients are moistened. (Do not overbeat or the muffins will toughen.)

Place lightly greased muffin pans in preheated oven until hot. Remove from oven and fill each muffin tin about two-thirds full with batter. Bake in the middle of oven for about 15 minutes or until rounded and browned on top.

Remove from oven and dot muffins with butter. Serve hot.

Makes about 24 muffins

SWEET POTATO PIE

1 recipe pâte brisée (see appendix)
2 large sweet potatoes, scrubbed
3 eggs, lightly beaten
½ cup sugar
1 tablespoon grated orange zest
1 tablespoon vanilla extract
1½ teaspoons ground nutmeg
¼ cup condensed milk

On a lightly floured surface, roll out pastry dough to a ⅛-inch thick round, 10 inches in diameter. Press into a 9-inch pie pan, prick bottom and sides with a fork, crimp edges, and refrigerate for 30 minutes.

Place sweet potatoes in a large pot of boiling water, cover and boil over medium heat for 20 minutes or until fork-tender.

Preheat oven to 350 degrees.

Drain potatoes and peel while warm. Place in a large mixing bowl and mash with a fork. Add eggs, sugar, orange zest, vanilla, and nutmeg and blend well. Gradually stir in condensed milk. Mixture should have the consistency of custard.

Pour sweet potato mixture into chilled pastry shell and place in the center of oven. Bake for 40 to 45 minutes or until lightly browned. Serve hot or cold with whipped cream or ice cream.

Makes 6 to 8 servings

PECAN PIE

1 recipe pâte brisée (see appendix)
2 eggs, beaten
1 cup light corn syrup
¼ teaspoon salt
1 tablespoon vanilla extract
1 tablespoon butter extract
½ cup firmly packed light brown sugar
½ cup granulated sugar
1 cup coarsely broken unsalted pecans
2 tablespoons butter, melted

On a lightly floured surface, roll out pastry dough to a ⅛-inch thick round, 10 inches in diameter. Press into a 9-inch pie pan, prick bottom and sides with a fork, and crimp edges. Refrigerate for 30 minutes.

Preheat oven to 300 degrees.

In a large mixing bowl, combine eggs, syrup, salt, vanilla, butter extract, brown and granulated sugars and blend well. Add pecans and blend. Pour mixture into chilled pastry shell. Drizzle melted butter over the top of pie. Place in oven and bake for 45 minutes. Let cool. Serve with whipped cream.

Makes 6 to 8 servings

Note: If using salted pecans, omit salt.

Overleaf: Dense and rich, Pecan and Sweet Potato Pies make the choice difficult.

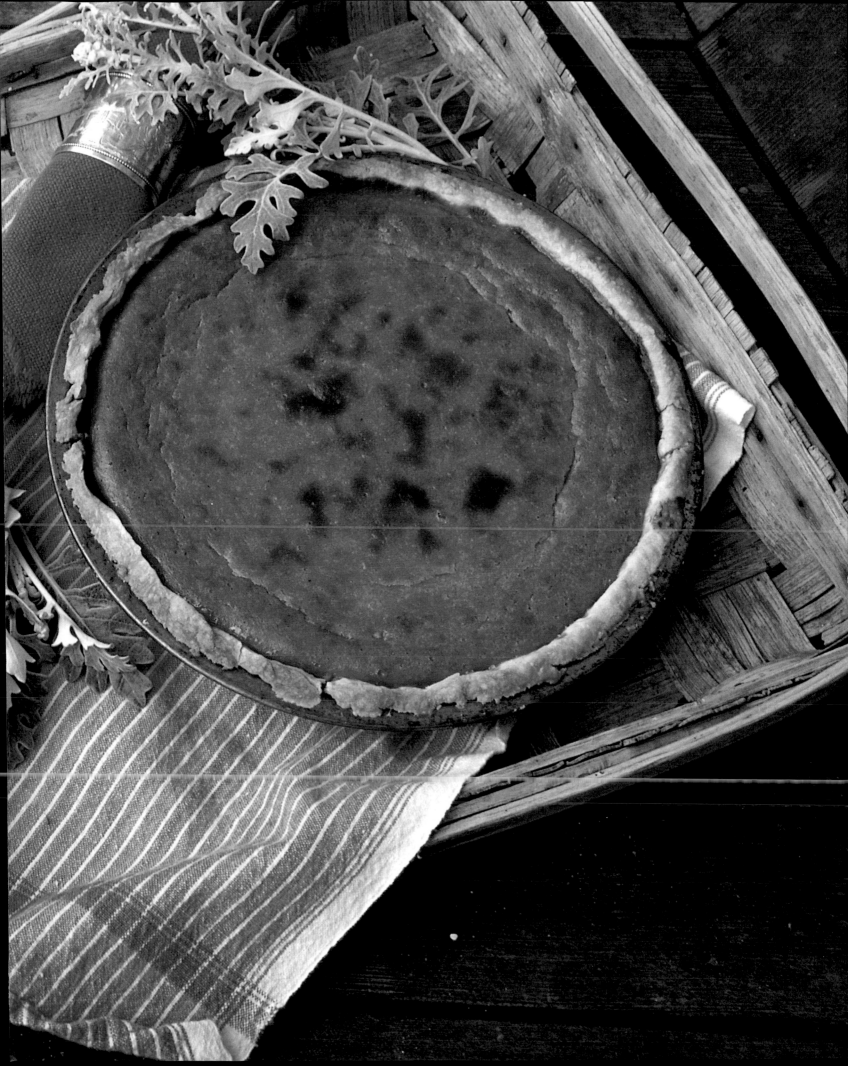

S Q U A T T E R S' R I G H T S

GOLDEN GATE
DINNER

LOBSTER CHOWDER

VEAL TONGUE SALAD WITH BLACK-EYED PEAS

VEGETABLE CHOW-CHOW

CONCORD GRAPE SORBET WITH CHOCOLATE
GRAPES AND MACAROON LEAVES

If the diverse reasons for outdoor entertaining could be reduced to a single common denominator, our instinct for homesteading might prove to be at the heart of this pursuit. "Taming the unknown," a more romantic generation might have called it. As latter-day adventurers, we set out equipped with blankets and makeshift tables to find a suitable spot for our portable feasts. And whether the event is a summer picnic on the beach or a bracing cookout by a snowbound ski trail, a proprietary mood animates every outdoor excursion: we linger, pass food and drink, and for a few hours, the scene becomes ours.

For Mr. and Mrs. Barry Traub of Vallejo, California, a shared passion for entertaining *en plein air* aroused the desire to construct a permanent passageway to the surrounding environment that would combine the beauty of natural ambience with the creature comforts of home. The idea required a partial renovation of their late-Victorian house, situated on a high hill affording a panoramic view of San Francisco, forty-five miles east across the Mare Island Channel. The Traubs' addition, a rectangular-shaped, glass-enclosed terrace, gives the illusion of dining out-of-doors. To enhance the primacy of the surrounding landscape, the terrace's interior has been left sparse. The floors and walls are an undiverting matte black, and large plants provide the sole accents of color.

The Traubs prefer entertaining on an intimate scale, and this evening they have invited another couple to share an autumn harvest dinner. As a late September dusk paints bands of brilliant orange across the sky, the friends are welcomed on the terrace where the table is set.

Collectors of fine china and unusual service pieces, the Traubs enjoy combining old and new objects in table settings that reflect their eclectic taste. For this occasion, white restaurant-ware soup dishes, delicate green majolica underplates, oversize white service plates, and French silver are set against a simple white cotton cloth and elegant, 36-inch damask napkins. Three purple agapanthus cut from the garden are arranged in elongated chemical beakers, mirror-images of the flowers' naturally bulbous form. This spare centerpiece permits an unobstructed view of the setting; from this high perspective the town is a jigsaw of stuccoed façades and flat roofs sloping down to the shoreline. In the distance, the spans of the Golden Gate Bridge glitter in the water.

Tonight's meal is prepared by Bradley Ogden, chef of Campton Place in San Francisco and one of the dynamic young turks of the new American cuisine. Ogden, a friend of the Traubs, has selected some of the specialties from the restaurant for this evening's dinner. For this Michigan native, the wholesome cooking of his native Midwest supplied a culinary basis in home-style preparations made with local ingredients. After years of professional training and experience, Ogden has gone on to refine traditional recipes and establish a creative multi-regional repertoire using newly cultivated ingredients such as fresh native sturgeon, exotic wild mushrooms, and free-range chickens. His light, deceptively simple style permits the natural flavors of fresh, excellent quality ingredients to prevail.

The dinner begins with Lobster Chowder —tender, firm chunks of claw and tail meat in a rich fish stock with sherry, bacon, and potatoes. It's served with golden cornsticks and slices of whole wheat bread and accompanied by a mellow Simi Chardonnay. The main course is an unusual salad based on a homely staple of Southern cooking, black-eyed peas. It includes veal tongue that is simmered in advance, then chilled. At serving time the tongue is sliced and arranged on a bed of chicory, red onion rings, and hot, cooked peas and dressed with a basil–pine nut sauce.

When the Septembers of earlier decades yielded their crops, farm wives would set aside time to pickle for the winter. Wax beans, peppers, onions, and other produce were mixed with salt brine, mustard seeds, and spices to make a concoction known as "chow-chow." Ogden's adaptation for tonight, served with the Veal Tongue Salad, is a colorful mix of red, yellow, and green peppers, baby carrots, and onion, all crisp-tender and subtly spiced. A full-bodied California Cabernet Sauvignon is a good complement.

Next to the table, a tall terra cotta planter filled with ice serves as a dramatic cooler for bottles of Schramsberg Champagne, poured as dessert is served. Deep purple scoops of Concord Grape Sorbet are mounded into compotes next to fanciful clusters of chocolate-dipped grapes and macaroon leaves.

A small dinner party for close friends offers an excellent opportunity for warm, personal entertaining. Begin with a menu that is simple yet imaginative; fewer courses are easier on the cook and can be just as effective as a larger variety of dishes. In Ogden's menu, a hot, rich first course provides a dramatic opening for the lighter, cold entrée. To avoid spending excessive time in the kitchen, plan on serving dishes that can be prepared mainly in advance. The elements of Ogden's main course and dessert can be made the day before and quickly assembled just before serving. Only the Lobster Chowder remains to be prepared the day of the dinner.

This casual and robust menu employs heritage recipes refined by imaginative innovations in technique, ingredients, and presentation. In its mixture of the naïve and the sophisticated, tonight's dinner acknowledges the vista beyond the terrace, the paradox of mountains and city lights that is the American landscape.

Overleaf: Glass walls afford a spectacular panorama, while within, the aroma of Lobster Chowder casts its own spell.

Lobster Chowder, accompanied by Simi Chardonnay.

LOBSTER CHOWDER

STOCK:
- **3** 1- to 1¼-pound lobsters, freshly killed
- **1** cup olive oil
- **1** cup coarsely chopped carrots
- **1** cup coarsely chopped celery
- **1** cup coarsely chopped onions
- **4** cups chicken stock or broth
- **1** cup dry sherry
- **8** sprigs parsley
- **4** bay leaves
- **2** teaspoons whole black peppercorns
- **8** sprigs fresh thyme, or 1 teaspoon dried

CHOWDER:
- **¼** cup finely diced salt pork, rind removed
- **2** slices bacon, cut into ¼-inch dice
- **2** cups diced celery

- **2** cups diced onion
- **1** tablespoon chopped fresh thyme leaves, or ½ teaspoon dried
- **¼** cup flour
- **2** cups heavy cream
- **2** cups peeled, coarsely diced Idaho potatoes, blanched in lightly salted water
- **1** tablespoon coarse salt
- **⅛** teaspoon cayenne pepper
- **½** teaspoon freshly ground white pepper

TO SERVE:
  Chopped parsley
- **8** to 10 teaspoons sweet butter

Break claws off lobsters, remove tails and set aside, keeping carcasses at hand to start stock. Heat oil in a large pot over high heat until it begins to smoke. Add carcasses and sauté until shells turn a deep red, about 4 minutes. Add carrots, celery, and onions and sauté for 5 to 8 minutes, or until they soften and turn a rich golden color. Add stock, sherry, parsley, bay leaves, peppercorns, and thyme, bring to a boil over medium-high heat, and skim foam from surface. Reduce heat to medium and simmer for 35 minutes. Strain stock through a fine sieve, discarding vegetables and carcasses. Return stock to the pot and bring to a simmer over medium-low heat. Add lobster claws and tails and simmer for 8 to 10 minutes, or until meat is just cooked. Remove from heat, strain stock, and set claws and tails aside to cool.

In a large, clean pot, sauté salt pork and bacon over medium heat until fat is rendered and meat is lightly browned and crisp. Add celery and onion and sauté for 4 minutes. Stir in thyme and flour to make a roux, and cook over low heat, stirring constantly, for about 5 minutes. Gradually add lobster stock, stirring constantly. Stir in cream, potatoes, salt, cayenne, and white pepper.

Remove meat from claws and tails and cut into ½-inch cubes. To serve, arrange lobster pieces in individual warmed shallow soup plates or bowls, ladle hot chowder over lobster, and garnish each with chopped parsley and 1 teaspoon butter.

Makes 8 to 10 servings

VEAL TONGUE SALAD WITH BLACK-EYED PEAS

BLACK-EYED PEAS:
- **2** ribs celery, coarsely chopped
- **1** carrot, coarsely chopped
- **½** medium white onion, coarsely chopped
- **4** cloves garlic, crushed
- **1** teaspoon black peppercorns
- **6** sprigs fresh thyme, or ½ teaspoon dried
- **2** bay leaves
- **1¼** cups dried black-eyed peas, soaked over-night in water
- **1** smoked ham hock
- **4** cups chicken stock

DRESSING:
- **2** tablespoons mustard seeds
- **¾** cup cider vinegar
- **2** tablespoons sugar
- **3** tablespoons shallots, thinly sliced
- **1** teaspoon freshly ground black pepper
- **½** cup olive oil
- **½** teaspoon coarse salt

TO SERVE:
- **1** small red onion, thinly sliced
- **1** small bunch chicory, torn into 2-inch pieces
- **2** pickled veal tongues (recipe follows)
- **1** cup basil–pine nut dressing (recipe follows)

To cook the peas, place celery, carrot, onion, garlic, peppercorns, thyme, and bay leaves on a large piece of clean cheesecloth and tie up securely to make a bouquet garni. Combine black-eyed peas, ham hock, stock, and bouquet garni in a large pot or Dutch oven and simmer over medium heat until peas are tender, about 20 minutes. Drain peas, discarding ham hock and bouquet garni. Spread peas on a baking sheet to cool quickly.

To make the dressing, combine mustard seeds, vinegar, and sugar in a small saucepan, and simmer over low heat for about 10 minutes, or until mustard seeds are tender. Remove from heat and let cool. Stir in shallots, pepper, oil, and salt.

In a large mixing bowl, combine peas, red onion, and chicory, pour dressing over them and toss well.

Divide salad among 4 individual serving plates. Cut tongues in ⅛-inch slices and arrange 5 to 6 slices on each plate over black-eyed pea salad without completely covering salad. Spoon about 2 tablespoons basil–pine nut dressing diagonally over tongue slices on each plate.

Serve with Vegetable Chow-Chow (see page 75) on the side.

Makes 4 servings

Pickled Veal Tongue

- **¼** cup white vinegar
- **3** cups chicken stock or broth
- **1½** cups dry white wine
- **2** tablespoons pickling spice
- **6** sprigs parsley
- **2** teaspoons black peppercorns
- **¾** cup coarsely chopped carrots
- **¾** cup coarsely chopped celery
- **¾** cup coarsely chopped onions
- **5** cloves garlic, crushed
- **⅛** teaspoon cayenne pepper
- **1** teaspoon coarse salt
- **1** lemon, cut in half
- **1** tablespoon mustard seeds
- **2** 5- to 7-ounce veal tongues

In a large stainless steel saucepan, combine vinegar, stock, wine, pickling spice, parsley, peppercorns, carrots, celery, onions, garlic, cayenne, salt, lemon, and mustard seeds and simmer for 20 minutes. Add tongues and simmer uncovered over medium heat for 30 to 35 minutes, or until tongues are tender.

Turn off heat and let tongues cool in cooking liquid. When cool enough to handle, remove from liquid and peel off outer membrane with a sharp knife. Return tongues to liquid and refrigerate until ready to slice.

Makes 4 servings

Basil–Pine Nut Dressing

½	cup tightly packed fresh basil leaves
½	cup pine nuts
1	tablespoon minced garlic
¼	cup olive oil
¼	cup freshly grated Parmesan cheese
2	tablespoons red wine vinegar
¼	cup mayonnaise
½	teaspoon freshly ground black pepper
¼	teaspoon coarse salt

Combine basil, pine nuts, and garlic in a food processor or electric blender and process until puréed. Transfer purée to a small mixing bowl, stir in the oil, Parmesan, vinegar, mayonnaise, pepper, and salt and blend well. Serve with Veal Tongue Salad.

Makes about 2 cups

VEGETABLE CHOW-CHOW

½	medium red pepper, cut into 1-inch pieces
½	medium yellow pepper, cut into 1-inch pieces
¼	medium green pepper, cut into 1-inch pieces
12	baby carrots, scraped
½	red onion, thinly sliced

DRESSING:

1½	cups cider vinegar
½	cup sugar
⅛	teaspoon cayenne pepper
1	teaspoon dried red chili flakes
2	teaspoons paprika
2	teaspoons coarse salt

Blanch peppers and carrots in a large saucepan of lightly salted boiling water just until tender, about 1 minute. Drain vegetables and plunge immediately into cold water to retain their color. Drain thoroughly and add onion slices.

In a small saucepan, combine vinegar, sugar, cayenne, chili flakes, paprika, and salt and simmer over medium heat until reduced by a third. Let cool slightly and pour over vegetables. Cover tightly and refrigerate overnight. Serve with Veal Tongue Salad.

Makes 4 servings

A far cry from farm fare, this version of Black-Eyed Peas accompanies slices of Pickled Veal Tongue and Vegetable Chow-Chow.

CONCORD GRAPE SORBET WITH CHOCOLATE GRAPES AND MACAROON LEAVES

SORBET:
- **2** pounds Concord grapes, stems removed
  Juice of 1 lemon
- **6** tablespoons sugar

CHOCOLATE GRAPES:
- **6** ounces semisweet chocolate
- **1** pound Concord grapes, stems removed

MACAROON LEAVES:
- **3** ounces almond paste
- **2** egg whites
- **⅔** cup sugar
- **¼** cup flour

In a large saucepan, combine grapes, 1 cup water, lemon juice, and 6 tablespoons sugar and bring to a boil over medium-high heat. Remove from heat and refrigerate overnight.

In a medium saucepan, melt chocolate, stirring, over hot, not boiling, water until just melted; do not allow chocolate to become too hot. Remove from heat.

Separate and thoroughly dry grapes. Using a sharp, sturdy wooden pick, dip each grape into the melted chocolate, turning to coat well. Drop coated grapes into neat clusters of about 8 grapes each on a baking sheet lined with aluminum foil. Refrigerate grapes until chocolate has hardened, overnight if possible.

In a small mixing bowl, combine almond paste and egg whites and blend until smooth. Stir in sugar and flour and blend well. Spread mixture very thinly onto a well-greased baking sheet and cut out into 6 leaf shapes. If you prefer, outline leaf shapes first on parchment paper and spread mixture over parchment. Use the tip of a sharp knife to outline veins on leaves. Carefully remove the leaves from the parchment with a metal spatula.

Purée chilled sorbet mixture in a food processor or food mill. Process in a sorbet or ice cream machine according to manufacturer's instructions and chill until ready to serve.

To serve, place grape clusters onto chilled individual dessert plates. Place two small scoops of sorbet on top of each cluster. Arrange a macaroon leaf on one side of each plate.

Makes 6 servings

Chef Ogden's dessert of fresh Concord grapes served with mounds of tart, refreshing Concord Grape Sorbet and shortbread cookies.

C H A P T E R

SIX

D O W N S T R E A M   A D R I F T

CANOE TRIP BARBECUE

LUNCH

CONFIT DE CANARD (PRESERVED DUCK LEGS)

RATATOUILLE

FRESH FRUIT AND CHEESE

DINNER

RED PEPPER SOUP

AIGUILLETTES DE CANARD AU POIVRE VERT
(SLICED DUCK BREASTS WITH GREEN
PEPPERCORN SAUCE)

GRILLED ZUCCHINI

GRILL BREAD

FLAMBEED CREPES WITH PEARS

After a healthy rain, the Delaware River spreads out luxuriously for miles of pure, clear water. Along the banks, weeds and tall grass grow in the rich soil, and overhead the blue sky unfurls cloudlessly. It is mid-morning in Milford, Pennsylvania, and noted New York cooking instructor Peter Kump has arrived with a group of five friends for a two-day, "getting away from it all" canoe trip. Their excursion will include several hours of paddling on the serene river, camping, and cooking outdoors amid the pine forests and purple hills of this picturesque region.

For Kump, as for a growing number of sports enthusiasts, strenuous exercise rewarded by the comforts of a fine meal offers the best of both worlds on vacation. As he comments: "Canoeing, camping, and good eating complement each other very well. After a few hours of morning canoeing everyone is hungry and tired. We'll have a break for lunch, then resume for a few hours. By this time it's 5 P.M. and the canoeing is over. What do you do for the rest of the night?" What Kump and his friends like to do is make an elaborate evening meal that will stretch for hours of cooking and eating until it is time to retreat to sleeping bags.

According to Kump, advance planning, organization, and "a prayer for good weather" are the necessary requirements for a successful canoe excursion. Preparations began days in advance with menu plans for the meals that will be served during the trip —lunch, dinner, and breakfast the next morning, and a variety of high-energy snacks and beverages. After the items for the menu had been determined, the storage of the food to preserve its freshness and logistics of transportation had to be dealt with. "Correct packing of food and planning of equipment necessary for cooking are essential," says Kump. He makes a complete list down to the last potholder and spatula he will need. He has prepared as much as possible in advance, then frozen the completed dishes in insulated storage containers. The food is frozen to retain its best flavor; but the frozen items also serve to keep the inside of the styrofoam coolers cold for everything else. All foods are then placed into the coolers in reverse order of the menu sequence so that the dishes for the first meal are on top. To prevent total loss if the canoe capsizes, the coolers are secured with ropes, then wrapped in waterproof survival blankets.

After two hours of downstream paddling, the group chooses a small inlet lined with rocks and fragrant with wildflowers for the picnic site. On shore, one of the canoes is overturned to serve as a bench. The waterproof blankets are spread on the ground for tablecloths; and lightweight enamel dishes that can be rinsed in the river, paper napkins, and plastic eating utensils are passed. The lunch menu includes a colorful Ratatouille, fragrant

Roughing it in style means a centerpiece of wildflowers, enamel plates and for dinner, tender Sliced Duck Breasts with Green Peppercorn Sauce, sautéed potatoes, and Grilled Zucchini, all washed down with a Beaujolais.

with oil and garlic. It is served with a classic Duck Confit, a specialty from the southwest of France that features sections of poultry cured in a salty brine and cooked in rendered duck fat until tender. The meat is then packed into jars, covered with fat, and preserved for later use. This confit is made with the legs of the birds whose succulent breasts will be grilled and served for the evening meal.

Gruyère cheese and fresh fruits follow. For beverages there are fruit juices, with plenty more for later on in the day.

After lunch, the group resumes its river journey. Several hours later, as the sun begins to dip gradually below the horizon, the canoers head for a campsite on the pebbled beach of Dingman's Ferry. For dinner, Kump has planned an elaborate barbecue. His assis-

CONFIT DE CANARD
(Preserved Duck Legs)

4	tablespoons salt
4	shallots, minced
3	tablespoons minced parsley
½	teaspoon dried thyme, crumbled
1	bay leaf, crumbled
2	teaspoons crushed white peppercorns
6	duck legs (or legs and wings from three 5-pound ducks)
8	cups rendered duck, goose, chicken, or pork fat
1	head garlic, halved and stuck with 2 cloves

In a small bowl, combine salt, shallots, parsley, thyme, bay leaf, and peppercorns. Cut legs into drumsticks and thighs, and wipe all pieces dry with a clean kitchen towel. Roll each piece in the herb mixture to coat thoroughly, and pack into a large earthenware crock or glass container large enough to hold all pieces. Sprinkle with remaining herb mixture, cover loosely, and store in refrigerator or a cool place for 24 to 48 hours.

Remove duck pieces from the herb mixture and wipe clean with a towel. Heat the rendered fat in a large, deep enameled kettle or Dutch oven. Carefully add duck pieces, ½ cup water, and garlic. There should be enough fat to cover duck pieces completely. Bring the fat to a boil over medium-high heat; reduce heat to low and simmer, uncovered, for 1½ to 2 hours (fat should not boil, but simmer gently over a heat just strong enough to ripple the surface), until duck flesh is tender and easily pierced with a wooden skewer.

Remove and drain duck pieces. Strain fat through a sieve lined with several layers of cheesecloth. Return strained fat to the kettle and boil to clarify, skimming surface frequently to remove any debris. Strain through sieve lined with clean cheesecloth and let fat cool to room temperature.

Meanwhile, pack duck pieces back into the crock or divide them among smaller glass or earthenware containers. Pour enough of the strained duck fat into each container to cover duck pieces completely. (Reserve any unused fat for cooking.) Cover containers with plastic wrap or tight-fitting lids and store in refrigerator or a cool place (such as a cold cellar) until ready to use. The flavor will be best if you allow the confit to rest for at least 1 month before using. It can be kept for up to 6 months in the fat.

To serve the confit, remove duck pieces from the fat and wipe clean with a towel. Preheat oven to 350 degrees and warm duck pieces on a rack in a roasting pan for 15 to 20 minutes. To finish, transfer to a skillet and sauté over medium-high heat for about 5 minutes on each side, until browned. Alternatively, allow the confit to come to room temperature, slice, and serve.

Makes 6 servings

RATATOUILLE

⅔ cup olive oil
1 pound onions, thickly sliced
1 pound mixed green, red, and yellow peppers, seeded and cut into 1-inch squares
1 pound small eggplant, peeled and cut into 1-inch squares
6 cloves garlic, chopped
1 teaspoon salt
Pinch cayenne pepper
2 pounds firm, ripe tomatoes, peeled, seeded, and cut into 1-inch squares
1 tablespoon dried thyme
Bouquet garni of parsley stems and 1 bay leaf
1 pound small zucchini, peeled and cut into 1-inch squares
½ cup chopped parsley leaves

Heat ⅓ cup of the oil in a large enameled pot or Dutch oven, add onions, and sauté over medium heat until softened, 5 to 8 minutes. Add peppers, eggplant, garlic, salt, and cayenne and sauté, stirring occasionally, over medium heat for about 10 minutes. Add tomatoes, thyme, and bouquet garni, reduce heat to very low and simmer, stirring occasionally, for about 1 hour. Stir in zucchini and continue to simmer slowly, partially covered, for 1 hour longer.

Ladle off and reserve excess liquid; continue to simmer vegetables over low heat. Pour reserved liquid into a small saucepan and simmer over medium heat until reduced to about ¾ cup.

Remove kettle from heat, add remaining ⅓ cup oil, ¼ cup of the parsley, and the reduced vegetable liquid. Correct seasoning if necessary. Let cool to room temperature. Sprinkle with remaining parsley before serving.

Makes 6 servings

Note: This recipe is adapted from Richard Olney's original.

RED PEPPER SOUP

4 tablespoons butter
1 pound leeks, washed, trimmed, and chopped
2 large red peppers, roasted, peeled, seeded, and quartered
3 medium potatoes (about 1 pound), peeled and diced
Salt
Freshly ground black pepper
5 tablespoons heavy cream

TO SERVE:
Julienne strips of leek

In a large stainless steel kettle or Dutch oven, melt butter over medium heat, add leeks and sauté, stirring, for about 10 minutes; do not allow them to brown. Add peppers, potatoes, and 8 cups water, and season with salt and pepper. Simmer, partially covered, for at least 40 minutes.

Scoop out vegetables with a slotted spoon and pass through a food mill or process in a food processor until smooth. Return puréed vegetables to the kettle, correct seasoning if necessary, add cream and cool. Serve hot or cold, garnished with julienne strips of leek.

Makes 6 servings

Duck breasts grill to succulence over the fire.

AIGUILLETTES DE CANARD AU POIVRE VERT
(Sliced Duck Breasts with Green Peppercorn Sauce)

1   cup white wine
⅓   cup Armagnac or Cognac
3   tablespoons brine from canned or bottled
     green peppercorns
½   cup chicken stock
1   cup crème fraîche (see appendix) or heavy
     cream
    Salt
2   tablespoons red wine vinegar
1   teaspoon sugar
3   tablespoons port
2   tablespoons green peppercorns
3   teaspoons minced, roasted, peeled, and
     seeded green pepper

3   duck breasts, split, skinned, and boned
     (from three 5-pound ducks)
    Freshly ground black pepper

Combine the wine and brandy in a medium saucepan and boil over medium-high heat until liquid has reduced by two-thirds. Add peppercorn brine and chicken stock and boil for 5 minutes more. Reduce heat slightly, add crème fraîche and salt, and let simmer at a very slow boil until sauce reduces by one-third, about 15 minutes.

Meanwhile, in a small saucepan, combine vinegar, sugar, and port and boil over high heat until mixture becomes syrupy and a deep caramel color, about 1 minute. Add to crème mixture, stir in peppercorns and green pepper, and blend well. Keep warm over a very low heat while preparing duck breasts.

Season duck breasts on both sides with salt and pepper, place under a hot broiler or on a grill over hot coals, and cook to desired doneness; 4 to 5 minutes per side for medium rare. Transfer duck breasts to a wooden cutting board and let rest for about 2 minutes. Using a sharp knife, cut breasts at an angle into thin, crosswise slices. Arrange slices in a fan on individual serving plates and spoon warm green peppercorn sauce over them. Serve immediately.

Makes 6 servings

Note: This dish is a nouvelle cuisine "classic," and this particular version is based on the recipes of Michel Guérard and Jacques Cagna.

GRILLED ZUCCHINI

1½   pounds zucchini (each about 2 inches in diameter), scrubbed
3   tablespoons vegetable oil
   Salt
   Freshly ground black pepper

Thoroughly dry zucchini, remove stem ends, and cut into lengthwise slices about ¼-inch thick. Pour oil into a sturdy plastic bag, add zucchini slices and close tightly. Shake to coat all zucchini pieces evenly with oil.

Lay zucchini slices on a grill 2 to 3 inches from hot coals and let cook, turning occasionally, for 5 to 7 minutes, until evenly browned on both sides. Sprinkle with salt and pepper and serve hot.

Makes 6 servings

GRILL BREAD

½   package (about ½ tablespoon) active dry yeast
3½   to 4 cups flour
1   tablespoon salt

Place 1 cup lukewarm water in a large mixing bowl and sprinkle the surface with yeast; let dissolve for 3 to 5 minutes. Add about 1 cup of the flour and stir with a wooden spoon until well blended. Let batter sit in a warm place, covered, for about 1 hour, until spongy.

Add salt and enough of the remaining flour to make a stiff dough. Sprinkle dough lightly with flour and knead, adding more flour if necessary, until satiny and elastic, about 10 minutes. Place in a large plastic bag and set aside in a warm place to rise until doubled in bulk, about 2 hours.

Turn dough out onto a lightly floured surface, punch down and knead for about 2 minutes. Return dough to plastic bag and let rise again until doubled. Form dough into a loaf and place on a lightly floured surface; let rise until doubled in bulk.

Place on a grill over hot coals, or on a hot griddle or skillet brushed with oil, and cook for about 20 minutes. Turn and cook for 20 minutes longer.

Makes 1 loaf

The sliced pears are sautéed in butter and sugar.

FLAMBEED CREPES WITH PEARS

½ cup sweet butter, softened
¾ cup firmly packed dark brown sugar
½ teaspoon ground cinnamon
6 large ripe pears, cored, peeled, and sliced
12 6½-inch crêpes (recipe follows)
½ cup eau-de-vie de poire, or other pear
  brandy, dark rum, or Kirsch

Prepare the crêpes.

Combine butter, sugar, and cinnamon in a small mixing bowl and blend well. Heat mixture in a large skillet or chafing dish, stirring over medium heat until sugar has completely dissolved. Add pears and simmer until tender, about 10 minutes. (Time will vary with type of pears and their degree of ripeness.)

Fold crêpes in half, then in half again, forming neat wedges. Add folded crêpes to skillet one at a time, spooning sauce over the top of each, and arranging them in a single layer if possible.

Warm the liquor in a ladle or small pan over high heat for 20 seconds, then carefully ignite with a match and pour over the top of the crêpes. Gently shake the pan, stirring slowly with a wooden spoon for 2 to 3 minutes, until the flames go out.

Divide the crêpes and pears among 6 individual dessert plates, spoon sauce over the top of each, and serve immediately.

Makes 6 servings

Crêpes

1½ cups flour
3 large eggs
1 tablespoon sugar
¾ cup cold milk
3 tablespoons brandy, rum, or kirsch
5 tablespoons sweet butter, melted, plus 3
  tablespoons, melted, for sautéing crêpes

Combine flour, eggs, sugar, milk, ¾ cup water, brandy, and 5 tablespoons of the butter in a food processor or electric blender and process until smooth and well blended. Batter should resemble a thin pancake batter, just thick enough to coat a wooden spoon. If it seems too thick, stir in a little more cold milk. Refrigerate, covered, for at least 1 hour before making crêpes.

Brush a 6½- to 7-inch crêpe pan or iron skillet with some of the remaining melted butter and place over medium-high heat until just beginning to smoke. Lift off the heat, add 3 to 4 tablespoons of the batter, and quickly tilt skillet to coat bottom evenly with a thin film. (Pour off any excess batter.)

Return pan to the heat for 40 to 80 seconds, until bottom is lightly browned. Loosen crêpe from edges of skillet with a spatula; carefully lift and turn to brown the other side for 30 seconds. Slide crêpe onto a plate. Brush skillet with a little more butter, heat to just smoking, and proceed in same manner until all batter has been used. Place sheets of plastic wrap or waxed paper between crêpes to keep them from sticking together.

Crêpes can be kept warm in the oven over a dish of simmering water, or they can be made in advance and reheated when needed. They can also be wrapped tightly in plastic and foil and frozen for up to 10 months.

Makes about 30 crêpes

The reward for rising early is a sumptuous breakfast of country-style sausages, sizzling fried eggs, and hefty slices of Grill Bread.

S U N S E T   A N D   C O C K T A I L S

TERRACE
COCKTAIL PARTY

ANGELS ON HORSEBACK

BEEF SATE WITH PEANUT SAUCE

BLACK FOREST SANDWICHES

CHICKEN PARMESAN

CHIN'S FRIED WONTONS

CRAB MEAT SALAD IN SNOW PEA PODS

CRUDITES AND DIPPING SAUCES

CELERY ROOT REMOULADE
IN BELGIAN ENDIVE SPEARS

FILET OF BEEF ON BEARNAISE BREAD

LAMB CURRY IN CUCUMBER CUPS

SCALLOPS SEVICHE

LEMON SHRIMP

NIÇOISE CANAPES

PROSCIUTTO AND ASPARAGUS TIPS

STRAWBERRIES WITH CREME FRAICHE

The cocktail party is unique among home entertainments because typically it follows a standardized procedure: early evening, two hours, lots of drink, finger foods. Faced with this traditional format, a prospective host can either passively submit to the norm or treat the rules flexibly, as guidelines to accept or reject according to his or her own instinct for entertaining. And the result of selecting the latter course can prove to be an uncommonly good party, for host and guest alike.

Finding the unexpected touch that will bring a personal accent to her parties is one of the many talents of Buffy Birrittella. As vice president of Polo/Ralph Lauren, her professional and social roles often overlap and necessitate frequent entertaining. Since the demands on a fashion executive allow few moments for detailed party planning, Buffy enlisted the aid of a New York caterer, Gay Jordan of Bespoke Food, for a recent cocktail party.

It is a mellow spring evening and fifty guests have been invited to share cocktails and the view at sunset from Buffy's terraced Manhattan apartment. As the turreted rooftops and peaked towers of the city turn golden in the waning light, guests mingle within an aerie of country-style antique furniture and attractive table settings. Early this morning, an antique American oak trestle table was moved to the terrace to serve as buffet. Heirloom baskets and wine goblets, Shaker trays, and redware and yellowware bowls were assembled for serving pieces. Bright spring blossoms, ripe fresh strawberries overflowing from bowls, and a multicolor striped rag runner for the table introduce bright accents; Buffy has hand-fringed blue and white gingham check napkins for the table and to use as basket liners.

The subtle interplay of dramatic cityscape and fresh-scrubbed country oasis is complemented by the menu. Working closely with Buffy in order to understand and incorporate her tastes and entertaining style, Gay has devised an eclectic menu that includes both traditional cocktail party fare and more unusual items. Both hot and cold appetizers have been selected that capture the mood of spring with fresh flavors, ingredients, and textures. There are the light-as-air pastel tints of cool green cucumbers, pale scallops, blush pink shrimp marinated in lemon juice, and fresh endive and crisp yellow peppers for dipping into delicate herb sauces. Choices also include Angels on Horseback—a cocktail party favorite consisting of oysters wrapped in bacon, then grilled just until tender—and ethnic fare such as an aromatic Indian Lamb Curry with apples and cinnamon, and hot, spicy Indonesian Beef Saté served on skewers with a chunky Peanut Sauce.

In keeping with the hostess's highly developed visual sense, food presentation was a major factor in preparation. As Gay remarks,

A well-organized bar makes serving effortless.

"Food should appeal to the eye if it is to appeal to the palate," and choice of serving platters, composition, and garnishes should be carefully considered. Selecting from Buffy's extensive antique pottery and copperware collection, the caterer forms simple food arrangements, abundant yet clean and uncluttered. For garnish, she uses fresh flowers in a flamboyant mixture of colors and shapes that offers dramatic contrast to the food items. For example, red snapdragons set off black pumpernickel sandwiches of Brie and ham, bright pink gerber daisies are placed behind a horseshoe of Crabmeat Salad in Snow Pea Pods, and irises have been poised

Overleaf: A spectacular cocktail buffet framed by the cityscape of Manhattan.

against a bowl of golden Fried Wontons. Each decorative element works effectively for the single serving platter and also contributes to the overall tenor of the event, in this case sophisticated informality. Long after sunset, guests linger in the comfortable, relaxed ambience of Buffy's terrace, clustered in groups for conversation, food and drink, and a party that seemed to fall naturally into place.

Many locations are suitable for an outdoor cocktail party as long as there is convenient access to a kitchen or work area. An enclosed patio, a garden, an ample porch, can be transformed into attractive and comfortable environments with a little attention to decoration and table setting. In planning the event Gay Jordan advises, "Think like a caterer and start with a minutely detailed work strategy that begins with your market list and concludes with clean-up detail." Begin by estimating the amount and variety of appetizers necessary for the number of guests invited. For the average two-hour cocktail party figure on serving twelve to fifteen appetizers per person, with a total of six selections for groups of twenty to twenty-five, eight for larger parties of forty to forty-five people. A smaller selection of unusual items is more effective than an overabundance of typical dishes. Flavors should offer contrast from mild and subtle to spicy hot. Similarly, textures should be varied from crisp to silken smooth and creamy. Timing is important, particularly for the amateur cook, and items should include several that can be made totally in advance to allow free time for the few dishes that require last-minute work. In this regard, a combination of hot and cold dishes works best to reduce final preparation detail. Cold appetizers can be arranged on serving platters and conveniently stored in the refrigerator, to be brought out at serving time while eleventh-hour reheating of hot items occurs. For a menu of six appetizers, choose two hot and four cold items. For eight items, plan on three hot and five cold.

Whether the party is for ten or fifty guests, Gay emphasizes the importance of accurately assessing the number of hours necessary to complete all details of the occasion. "This is not a last-minute party, and appetizers are small, fussy items that need minute attention both in preparation and in presentation, so plan on having a block of time available on the day of the party. For the working host, a Saturday night or Sunday afternoon party offers the advantage of more preparation time." She also recommends having an extra pair of hands (an obliging friend or family member, for example) to help in the kitchen during the peak period of serving to make sure serving trays are replenished and attractive, to reheat warm items, to make certain there are enough clean glasses and ice, and in general to help ensure that the affair is running smoothly so that the host is not overwhelmed with responsibilities during the party.

Crab Meat Salad in Snow Pea Pods is dramatically set off by a black lacquer serving tray.

ANGELS ON HORSEBACK

2½   pounds sliced lean bacon (about 48 strips), separated and trimmed to 7-inch lengths

4   dozen medium fresh oysters, shucked, rinsed, and patted dry

Preheat oven to 450 degrees.

Lay bacon strips on a rack in a shallow baking dish and bake for about 7 minutes, until partially cooked but still pliable. Drain on paper towels and let cool slightly.

Place an oyster on one end of each bacon strip, roll up snugly, and pierce through with a toothpick to hold oyster and bacon securely in place. Refrigerate until just before serving time.

Preheat oven to 350 degrees.

Place about half the angels, or as many as will fit without crowding, on a rack in baking dish and bake for 5 to 7 minutes, turning once or twice until bacon is crisp and browned all around. Repeat with remaining pieces. Serve hot.

Makes 48 pieces

Note: These can be assembled the night before or on the morning of the party.

BEEF SATE WITH PEANUT SAUCE

3   tablespoons peanut oil
1   large onion, minced
1   2-inch piece fresh ginger root, peeled and minced
2   cloves garlic, minced
½   cup creamy peanut butter
2   tablespoons soy sauce
1   teaspoon sesame oil
1   teaspoon cayenne pepper
2   tablespoons brown sugar
    Grated zest of 1 lemon
2   pounds sirloin, flank, or sirloin tip steak, cut into 1-by-½-inch strips
1   cup peanut sauce (recipe follows)
1   bunch scallions, trimmed and cut into julienne strips

In a large skillet, heat the peanut oil. Add onion, ginger, and garlic and sauté over medium heat until softened. Stir in ½ cup water, peanut butter, soy sauce, sesame oil, cayenne, and brown sugar and simmer, stirring, for 3 minutes. Stir in lemon zest and let cool to room temperature.

Transfer to a shallow baking dish. Add sirloin strips and turn in the marinade to coat well. Cover and let marinate, refrigerated, for 24 hours.

Arrange sirloin strips on a broiler pan or baking sheet and cook under a hot broiler for 4 minutes, turning once. Pierce each strip with a toothpick, dab with peanut sauce and garnish with scallions. Serve warm.

Makes about 50 pieces

Note: Saté may be broiled for 2 minutes and pierced with toothpicks in advance, then warmed in a 450 degree oven for about 4 minutes just before garnishing and serving.

Peanut Sauce

½   cup chunky peanut butter
½   teaspoon cayenne pepper
1   tablespoon grated fresh ginger root
1   teaspoon soy sauce
2   tablespoons chopped scallions

In a mixing bowl, combine the peanut butter with ½ cup of water and whisk until smooth. Add the cayenne, ginger, and soy sauce and whisk until thoroughly blended. Sprinkle with scallions. Serve at room temperature with beef saté.

Makes 1 cup

BLACK FOREST SANDWICHES

1½   pounds ripe Brie, rind removed
1   4-ounce package cream cheese, softened
2   tablespoons sweet butter, softened
    Freshly ground black pepper
1   loaf party-size black bread, sliced into 50 thin slices
17   thin slices Black Forest ham, each cut into 3 pieces to fit size and shape of bread
1   bunch watercress, tough stems removed

In a food processor, combine Brie, cream cheese, and butter, season with pepper, and blend thoroughly.

Arrange bread slices in two rows of 25 on a flat work surface. Spread each slice with Brie mixture. Place two slices of ham on 25 of the bread slices, and top with a dab of the Brie mixture and a watercress sprig. Invert remaining 25 Brie-spread slices on top to make 25 sandwiches. Cut each in half diagonally to make 50 canapés. Cover with damp paper towels to keep from

A platter of Black Forest Sandwiches.

drying out and refrigerate until ready to serve.

Makes 50 canapés

Note: The Brie mixture can be made a day in advance and stored, covered, in the refrigerator. Allow it to soften to room temperature before assembling sandwiches the day of the event.

CHICKEN PARMESAN

4   whole chicken breasts, split, skinned, and boned
    Juice and grated zest of 2 lemons
4   cloves garlic, crushed
1   cup olive oil
    Pinch thyme
    Coarse salt
    Freshly ground white pepper
3   eggs, lightly beaten
1   to 2 cups fresh French bread crumbs
    Corn oil for frying
¼   cup freshly grated Parmesan cheese

Remove white tendon from each breast half and cut each breast into 6 to 8 bite-size pieces.

In a large shallow dish, combine lemon juice and zest, garlic, and olive oil, season with thyme, salt, and pepper, and stir until well blended. Place chicken pieces in the marinade and turn to coat well; let marinate, covered, overnight.

Remove chicken pieces from the marinade and set aside. Stir eggs into the marinade and blend well. Return chicken pieces to the dish and turn to coat well with the batter.

Place bread crumbs in a shallow bowl and roll chicken pieces in them until evenly coated.

Into a large heavy skillet, pour enough corn oil to fill by about half. Heat until a bread cube dropped in the hot oil sizzles and turns golden. Add the chicken pieces in small batches so that the oil does not cool down, and fry until golden brown, about 3 minutes. Adjust heat under skillet as needed to maintain a constant temperature.

Drain chicken pieces on paper towels, sprinkle with Parmesan cheese, and serve.

If preparing chicken in advance, drain and set aside in a cool place (but not in the refrigerator) until just before serving. Preheat the oven to 350 degrees, spread chicken pieces on a baking sheet and heat for about 5 minutes. Sprinkle with Parmesan cheese and serve in a napkin-lined basket.

Makes 50 to 60 pieces

Chin's Fried Wontons with dipping sauce.

CHIN'S FRIED WONTONS

½   pound lean ground pork
3   tablespoon grated fresh ginger root
5   scallions (white and tender green part), finely chopped
1   8-ounce can water chestnuts, drained and chopped
3   tablespoons soy sauce
½   package square wonton skins (about 50 skins) (see note)
1   egg yolk, beaten
3   to 4 cups vegetable oil for deep frying
1   cup wonton dipping sauce (recipe follows)

In a medium mixing bowl, combine pork, ginger, scallions, water chestnuts, and soy sauce, and blend together well.

Working with 6 to 8 wonton skins at a time to prevent them from drying out, separate skins and lay out on a flat surface. Place ½ teaspoon of pork mixture in the upper left corner of each skin. Fold over twice diagonally toward center of wonton; the second fold should fall on the diagonal center of skin. Brush lower corner of skin with egg yolk, bring corner up over filling and press firmly in place. Place, flap side down, on a baking sheet.

Pour oil to a depth of about 1½ inches in a wok or large, heavy skillet over high heat and heat to about 350 degrees. Carefully slip wontons into the hot oil, frying in batches and turning once or twice until lightly browned all over, about 2 to 3 minutes. Remove to paper towels and drain. Keep warm in a 250 degree oven while frying remaining wontons and serve hot with wonton dipping sauce.

Makes about 50 wontons

Note: Fresh wonton skins, found in Chinese groceries, are preferable. If those aren't available, use the packaged frozen skins. Wontons can be made several hours in advance, then reheated in a 350 degree oven for 5 to 7 minutes, until warmed through, or they can be made well in advance and frozen.

Wonton Dipping Sauce

1½	teaspoons dry Chinese mustard
½	cup bitter orange marmalade
1	tablespoon honey
1	tablespoon soy sauce

In a mixing bowl, combine mustard with just enough water to make a smooth paste. Stir in the marmalade, honey, and soy sauce and blend thoroughly.

Makes 1 cup

CRAB MEAT SALAD IN SNOW PEA PODS

50	unblemished, fresh young snow peas
¾	pound Maryland lump crab meat
½	large red pepper, cored, seeded, and minced
4	ribs celery, minced
2	tablespoons finely chopped parsley
¼	cup mayonnaise
1	tablespoon lemon juice
1	teaspoon grated lemon zest
	Salt
	Freshly ground black pepper

Remove stem ends and string the snow peas. Blanch in a large pot of rapidly boiling salted water for about 20 seconds. Plunge immediately in cold water to stop the cooking and preserve their color. Drain and pat dry.

Carefully pick over the crab meat to remove all shell and cartilage. Place in a mixing bowl with red pepper, celery, parsley, mayonnaise, lemon juice and zest, and season with salt and pepper. Mix together thoroughly.

Using a sharp knife, slit open the straight seam side of each pea pod, and with a small fork, fill each with about 1 teaspoon of crab meat mixture. Wipe outside of pods clean of any filling. Place them close together on a baking sheet lined with paper towels and refrigerate until ready to serve.

Makes 50 stuffed snow peas

Note: The crab mixture can be made the day before serving, and refrigerated, covered. The pea pods can be stuffed early in the day, wiped clean and arranged on paper towels without touching so they won't get limp.

CRUDITES AND DIPPING SAUCES

VEGETABLES FOR DIPPING:

Belgian endive, root ends removed and leaves separated
Whole red and white radishes
Whole red and yellow cherry tomatoes
Zucchini, cut into 3-by-¼-inch strips
Red, green, yellow, and purple peppers, cored, seeded, and cut into strips
Whole snow peas
Whole sugar snap peas
Whole haricots verts
Carrots, scraped and cut into 3-by-¼-inch strips
Fennel, trimmed and cut into strips
Asparagus spears, trimmed to about 4 inches
Cauliflower, broken into florets
Broccoli, broken into florets
Whole small white mushrooms
Whole enoki mushrooms
Jicama, peeled and cut into 3-by-¼-inch strips

DIPPING SAUCES:

Guacamole sauce (recipe follows)
Basil sauce (recipe follows)

Prepare your choice of any or all the vegetables and arrange them decoratively on a platter or in baskets. (Vegetables such as snow peas, sugar snap peas, haricots verts, carrots, asparagus, cauliflower, and broccoli should be blanched briefly before serving.)

Place the 2 dipping sauces in small bowls next to the vegetables. You will need approximately 2 cups of dipping sauce for 6 pounds of vegetables.

Guacamole Sauce

3   ripe avocados, peeled and pitted
1   medium yellow onion, chopped
    Juice of 2 limes
3   jalapeño or green chilies, seeded and chopped
1   clove garlic, chopped
2   tablespoons sour cream
1   ripe tomato, peeled, seeded, and chopped
    Salt
    Tabasco
2   teaspoons chopped fresh cilantro

Place 2 of the avocados in a food processor with the onion, lime juice, chilies, and garlic and process until puréed. Add sour cream and process to a thin dipping consistency, adding more sour cream if necessary.

Chop the remaining avocado finely and place in a large mixing bowl. Add the processed avocado mixture and tomato, season with salt and Tabasco to taste and blend together well. To prevent discoloration, place an avocado pit in the dip, cover, and chill until serving time. Just before serving, sprinkle chopped cilantro over the dip and surround with crudités and tostadas.

Makes 2 cups

Basil Sauce

3   cups fresh basil leaves, rinsed and patted dry
1   teaspoon olive oil
1½   cups mayonnaise, preferably homemade (see appendix)
     Dash Tabasco
     Dash Worcestershire sauce
1   tablespoon fresh lemon juice
     Coarse salt

Place the basil leaves and olive oil in a food processor and process until puréed. Add the mayonnaise, Tabasco, Worcestershire, lemon juice, and salt to taste, then process until thoroughly blended.

Makes 2 cups

CELERY ROOT REMOULADE IN BELGIAN ENDIVE SPEARS

3   medium celery roots, peeled and quartered
Juice and grated zest of 2 lemons
1   cup mayonnaise, preferably homemade (see appendix)
3   tablespoons Dijon-style mustard
Coarse salt
Freshly ground white pepper
12   4- to 5-inch heads Belgian endive
1   cup chopped parsley

Remove the pithy core from celery root and grate with the finest grating disk of a food processor, or by hand. Sprinkle with a little of the lemon juice and toss to prevent discoloration.

In a large mixing bowl, combine remaining lemon juice, zest, mayonnaise, and mustard, season to taste with salt and pepper, and whisk until thoroughly blended. Add grated celery root and toss. Add additional lemon juice and salt if needed. Refrigerate overnight, covered, to allow flavors to blend.

Just before serving, cut off the root ends of endive and separate leaves. Spread about 1 teaspoon of the remoulade mixture into the cupped side of each endive spear, filling about ⅓ full. Sprinkle each spear with a little chopped parsley, arrange spears in a spoke on a round platter, and serve.

FILET OF BEEF ON BEARNAISE BREAD

1½   pounds center cut of beef tenderloin, trimmed of fat and sinew, cut lengthwise into 2 equal pieces, and each half tied with string
1   teaspoon vegetable oil
1   teaspoon dried rosemary, crumbled
2   baguettes French bread, cut into 50 thin slices
1½   cups Béarnaise butter (recipe follows)

TO SERVE:
Coarse salt
Freshly ground black pepper
1   bunch parsley, chopped

Preheat oven to 425 degrees.

Rub tenderloin with oil and rosemary. Place one half on a rack in a roasting pan and roast in the center of the oven for about 15 minutes, or until a meat thermometer registers 120 degrees. Remove and let cool to room temperature. (Do not refrigerate.) Roast the other half in the same manner.

Spread bread slices with Béarnaise butter. Re-form slices, buttered sides together, into several small loaves and wrap in aluminum foil. (This way, they can be heated in small batches and served warm.)

Shortly before serving, preheat oven to 350 degrees. Place bread in oven as needed for 5 minutes until heated through. Meanwhile, remove string from tenderloin and slice into 50 thin slices. Remove bread from oven and place a slice of beef on each piece. Sprinkle with salt and pepper, and garnish with parsley. Serve immediately.

Makes about 50 pieces

Note: The Béarnaise bread can be made ahead, wrapped in loaves of 16 to 18 pieces, and frozen, to be removed and heated just before serving. The tenderloin can be cooked earlier in the day, cooled, and sliced a few hours in advance, but it should not be refrigerated.

Béarnaise Butter

½ cup dry vermouth
½ cup sherry vinegar
3 tablespoons minced shallots
1 tablespoon dried tarragon
½ teaspoon freshly ground black pepper
1½ cups sweet butter, chilled and cut into pieces
Salt

In a small saucepan, combine vermouth, vinegar, shallots, tarragon, and pepper and simmer over medium heat until liquid is almost evaporated. Let cool.

Place reduced mixture in a food processor with butter and process until smooth. Season with salt. Refrigerate, covered, until needed. Bring to room temperature before spreading.

Makes 1½ cups butter

LAMB CURRY IN CUCUMBER CUPS

2 thin seedless cucumbers, scored with a fork, and cut crosswise into ¼-inch slices
1 pound lean ground lamb
2 tablespoons butter
1 large onion, finely chopped
2 Granny Smith or other firm, tart apples, peeled, cored, and finely chopped
6 ribs celery, finely chopped
1 medium green pepper, cored, seeded, and finely chopped
3 tablespoons hot Indian curry powder
½ teaspoon ground cinnamon
½ teaspoon cayenne pepper
2 tablespoons flour
¾ cup chicken stock
¼ cup heavy cream
2 tablespoons Major Grey chutney, chopped
Salt

TO SERVE:
¼ cup shredded unsweetened coconut

Using a small melon baller, scoop out a pocket on one side of each cucumber round, being care-ful not to cut through cucumber. Drain, pocket side down, on a baking sheet lined with paper towels and refrigerate until ready to assemble.

In a large skillet, sauté lamb over medium heat, breaking up and stirring with a spoon until lightly browned. Transfer meat to a paper towel to drain. Pour off fat from skillet and wipe clean.

Melt butter in the skillet, add onion, apples, celery, and green pepper and sauté over low heat for about 3 minutes; vegetables should remain slightly crunchy. Stir in curry powder, cinnamon, cayenne, and flour and sauté 1 minute longer. Stir in stock, cream, chutney, and lamb. Season with salt and let simmer over low heat until mixture has thickened. Remove from heat and refrigerate until ready to assemble. The lamb mixture can be made 2 days in advance.

Just before serving, reheat lamb mixture until warmed through. Spoon a generous teaspoon of lamb into each cucumber cup, sprinkle a pinch of shredded coconut over each and serve immediately.

Makes about 50 pieces

SCALLOPS SEVICHE

18 sea scallops, each cut crosswise into 3 slices to make 54 thin slices
¼ cup Pernod
Juice of 2 limes
2 tablespoons minced shallots

2 teaspoons crushed drained green peppercorns
2 teaspoons sherry vinegar
2 seedless cucumbers, scored with a fork and thinly sliced

Skewers of Scallops Seviche.

TO SERVE:

  2 tablespoons chopped fresh cilantro
  2 tablespoons finely chopped red and green
      pepper

In a large skillet, place the scallop slices, Pernod, and enough water to cover and poach over low heat about 3 minutes, until opaque.

Combine lime juice, shallots, green peppercorns, and sherry vinegar in a mixing bowl. Drain scallops, add to the mixing bowl and toss in the dressing. Let marinate, refrigerated, overnight.

To assemble, reserve the marinade and pat scallops and cucumber slices dry on paper towels. Arrange cucumber slices in a single layer, top each with a scallop slice and spear with a wooden toothpick, so that the cucumber folds over the scallop slightly.

Dab the scallop and cucumber skewers with a little of the marinade and chill, covered with damp towels, until serving. Just before serving, sprinkle with a little chopped cilantro and red and green pepper. These skewers can be assembled up to 2 hours before serving.

Lemon Shrimp dotted with red pepper and fresh dill.

LEMON SHRIMP

50 medium fresh shrimp (16 to 20 per pound),
     peeled and deveined
     Juice and grated zest of 2 lemons
3 tablespoons Dijon-style mustard
3 cloves garlic, crushed
1 red onion, thinly sliced
1 cup olive oil
     Freshly ground white pepper
     Coarse salt
2 tablespoons finely chopped red pepper
2 sprigs fresh dill, chopped

Place the shrimp in a large saucepan, cover
with cold water and bring to a simmer over
medium-high heat; simmer until just pink, 5
to 8 minutes.

Meanwhile, in a mixing bowl, combine the
lemon juice and zest, mustard, garlic, and onion.
Gradually add the olive oil, whisking until thoroughly blended. Season to taste with pepper and
blend.

Drain the shrimp and toss while still warm in
the dressing. Let cool, cover, and refrigerate at
least 8 hours.

Before serving, pat shrimp dry and thread
long wooden toothpicks through the tail end and
into the top of each, making neat rounds. Season
lightly with salt and sprinkle with red pepper
and dill. Serve immediately, or chill, covered
with paper towels, until serving.

Makes 50 appetizers

NIÇOISE CANAPES

1½   pounds Niçoise olives, drained and pitted
1½   pounds pimiento-stuffed green olives,
       drained
½   cup mayonnaise
24   very thin slices whole wheat or white bread
12   thin slices soppersata or Genoa salami
12   thin slices provolone
12   thin slices mortadella

Place Niçoise olives in a food processor or electric blender and process with on/off turns until reduced to a mealy texture. Transfer to a mixing bowl. Process green olives in the same manner and add to mixing bowl. Add mayonnaise and blend thoroughly. The mixture should have the consistency of a thick spread; if it seems too stiff, add more mayonnaise.

To assemble, arrange bread slices in two rows of 12 on a flat surface, discarding any broken slices. Spread each slice with olive mixture. Layer the soppersata, provolone, and mortadella on 12 slices. Invert remaining 12 slices on top to make 12 sandwiches. Trim off crusts and cut in half diagonally twice to make 48 triangular canapés. To keep fresh, cover with dampened paper towels placed between 2 dry towels. Refrigerate until ready to serve.

Makes 48 canapés

Note: The spread can be made up to 5 days ahead and refrigerated, covered, until needed. The canapés can be made a day ahead.

PROSCIUTTO AND ASPARAGUS TIPS

50   fresh asparagus spears, trimmed to 3 inches
       (reserve the stalks for soup)
1   cup sweet butter, softened
     Grated zest of 1 lemon
1   tablespoon fresh lemon juice
17   thin slices prosciutto, each cut into 3 rectan-
       gles about 2-by-3 inches

In a large saucepan of boiling salted water, blanch the asparagus briefly and drain.

In a medium mixing bowl, combine butter, lemon zest, and juice and blend thoroughly. Lay the prosciutto slices out on a flat work surface and spread each slice with lemon butter. Place an asparagus tip on each piece of prosciutto and roll up securely, allowing the tip of the asparagus to extend slightly beyond the edge of the prosciutto. Trim the ends to uniform length and chill, covered with paper towels, until ready to serve.

STRAWBERRIES WITH CREME FRAICHE

2   cups crème fraîche (see appendix)
3   teaspoons superfine sugar
2   teaspoons Framboise
60   large, unblemished fresh strawberries,
       rinsed and drained
2   cups dark brown sugar

In a medium mixing bowl, combine the crème fraîche, superfine sugar, and Framboise and blend thoroughly. Spoon into a small serving bowl. Pile strawberries into a crystal or other decorative serving bowl and serve next to the crème fraîche and a small bowl of dark brown sugar for sprinkling over the berries.

FIRE AND ICE

PICNIC ON THE SKI SLOPES

Lunch

Beef Barley Soup

Chili

Irish Soda Bread

French Onion Saute

Indian Pudding

Chocolate Cheesecake

Hot Buttered Rum

Dinner

Shrimp Grilled with Hot Chili
Pepper Relish

Grilled Escargots

Sea Scallops Grilled with Lime Butter

Lobsters Grilled with Lemon Butter

Marinated Skewered Beef

Sweet Potatoes
Grilled with Orange Butter

Grilled Shiitake Mushrooms, Cucumber,
and Red Onion

Melted Raclette Cheese

Hot Spiced Wine

On a cold February morning in Jackson, New Hampshire, it's a rare vacationer who is not already awake and dressed for the slopes by six o'clock. For this small town in the northeast corner of the state is ski country, deep in the Mount Washington Valley of the White Mountains, and like neighboring villages, it attracts thousands of tourists who come in winter for its well-plotted ski trails, turn-of-the-century inns, antiques, and covered bridges. First-time visitors invariably take a ride on the nearby Conway Scenic Railroad, which pulls out from a station built in 1874 for a tour of the various attractions and ski facilities: Mount Cranmore with its thirteen downhill ski runs and fifteen-hundred-foot vertical drop; Wildcat, a few miles to the north, the most challenging slope in the area; and Tuckerman's Ravine where the absence of ski lifts makes the sport especially exhilarating—if you want to ski there you have to climb up the mountain on foot.

In addition to offering these impressive downhill runs, Jackson is the center of cross-country skiing for the North Conway region, and this morning the trail that snakes through the backyard of the Christmas Farm Inn is already dotted with early skiers of all ages. In the cozy dining room of the Inn, originally built in 1786, a group of friends, who have driven up from Boston for the weekend, lingers over scrambled eggs and coffee, coordinating plans for a day of skiing that will include a midday outdoor picnic and a lavish supper buffet.

Picnics in the snow are familiar sights here. Short winter days mean that trails get dark early, and for ski enthusiasts, bringing a lunch and eating beside the trail saves time and is also more fun than heading back to town; after a few hours of strenuous cross-country exercise, relaxing over a warm meal is a welcome, fortifying break.

Plans for today's ski picnic begin with the selection of the luncheon setting—a flat clearing close to a cluster of pines—where everyone will rendezvous after two hours of skiing. For less elaborate meals the food is distributed evenly among the skiers and carried in back packs. But today's menu is extensive, including fragile items, such as a cheesecake, so everything is packed into two large styrofoam containers—one for hot and the other for cold foods—then transported in a car by an Inn employee to the designated spot where the containers are left and covered with lightweight thermal reflector blankets.

At the appointed hour, the group gathers at the picnic site. The thermal blankets are spread over the snow to serve as moisture-resistant tablecloths, and plastic plates are passed. The hearty repast starts with mugs of a hot Beef Barley Soup, followed by serv-

Lunch on the ski trail: Irish Soda Bread, Indian Pudding, French Onion Sauté, Chili (on dinner plate), plus thermoses of Beef Barley Soup.

After lunch, skiers set out for an afternoon of exploring the trails.

ings of an incendiary Chili guaranteed to rouse the spirits of the most cold-benumbed picnicker. Wide-mouth thermoses keep the soups steaming hot, and other insulated containers keep the Irish Soda Bread and French Onion Sauté sandwiches warm. Both have been presliced to make eating them easier. With Hot Buttered Rum, who could ask for anything more for dessert than spicy Indian Pudding and wedges of silky Chocolate Cheesecake.

Fortified for the afternoon, the picnickers set off for a few more hours of exploring trails and more appetite-arousing exertion before the dinner buffet.

Upon returning to the lodge at nightfall, the hungry skiers warm up and quickly become cooks as preparations begin for what promises to be the climax of this active day. Bill and Sydna Zeliff, the owners of Christ-

mas Farm Inn, have constructed a temporary grill composed of a large oven rack set on top of cinder blocks in their central fireplace. It will be used for cooking tonight's menu.

Not the least of Jackson's attractions is its proximity to Maine, and this morning one of the Inn's employees has gone to a fish market just over the border and returned with a plentiful selection of seafood, including scallops, shrimp, and lobster. Since the meal is to be presented as a casual buffet, guests will make selections from the variety of marinated raw ingredients set out for them to thread onto metal and bamboo skewers and then do their own grilling. Tender sea scallops brushed with lime butter, a flavorful starting point for the dinner, need only a few minutes on the grill. Another quickly cooked first-course choice is jumbo shrimp tangy with the bite of hot pepper relish. One of the entrée selections, cubes of top sirloin marinated overnight in soy sauce, ginger, and garlic, adds an Oriental accent to the menu, particularly when accompanied by grilled shiitake mushrooms and cucumber chunks. Grilled lobsters are an indulgence affordable in Maine, but they can be omitted from the menu by simply increasing the amount of beef and serving it as the single entrée item. To complete the menu, sweet potatoes, precooked until tender, get a splash of orange juice before going on the grill for a quick searing.

The table setting and service are informal

Skis dry by the fire as dinner preparations begin.

and functional in keeping with the relaxed mood of this fireside buffet where friends take turns eating, cooking, and tending the fire. Oversize pottery dinner plates, simple eating utensils, heat-resistant glass mugs for hot mulled wine and spiced cider, and the welcoming ambience of a ski lodge in winter are the only other requirements for this evening's convivial tableau.

A little while later, a handsome wheel of raclette cheese is placed on a stone slab near the hearth, to melt down and be scraped off and spread on French bread for dessert along with ripe pears and apples. Conversation and hot spiced wine make good companions for the night; after a day of exercise it feels right just to rest for a while.

BEEF BARLEY SOUP

3   tablespoons butter
1   pound beef round or chuck, cut into
     1-inch cubes (see note)
     Salt
8   cups beef stock or consommé
1   large unpeeled potato, diced
1   cup diced onions
1   cup diced carrots
1   cup diced celery
1   cup diced fresh green beans
⅓   cup barley
1   bay leaf
1   cup sturdy, dry red wine
2   teaspoons freshly ground black pepper
3   tablespoons flour

Melt 1 tablespoon of the butter in a large pot or Dutch oven. Season beef with salt, place in the pot, and sauté over medium-high heat until lightly browned all over. Add about 2 cups of the beef stock, reduce heat to medium-low, cover, and simmer for about 1 hour, or until meat is cooked through and tender. Add remaining stock, potato, onions, carrots, celery, green beans, barley, bay leaf, ¾ cup of wine, and season well with salt and pepper. Simmer over medium-low heat until vegetables are cooked, about 20 minutes.

Melt remaining 2 tablespoons butter in a small skillet, add flour and cook, stirring constantly, over medium-low heat for 6 to 8 minutes. Stir flour-butter roux into soup, stirring constantly until soup is thick and creamy. Stir in remaining wine, correct seasoning if necessary, and serve.

Makes 6 to 8 servings

Note: Leftover beef is also very suitable for this soup. If beef has already been cooked, it does not need to be browned or simmered before adding vegetables.

CHILI

6   pequin chilies, seeds removed
6   ancho chilies, seeds removed
2   tablespoons olive oil
1   pound boneless stewing beef, cut into
     ½-inch cubes
1   pound boneless pork, cut into ½-inch
     cubes
1   28-ounce can Italian plum tomatoes,
     undrained
2   bay leaves
1   tablespoon cumin seed
2   cloves garlic
2   teaspoons oregano
2   tablespoons paprika
3   tablespoons chili powder
1   tablespoon sugar
     Coarse salt
     Freshly ground black pepper

Place chilies in a bowl, cover with 2 cups boiling water, and let soak at least 30 minutes. Drain, reserving the liquid, and set aside.

In a heavy saucepan, heat the oil, add the cubed beef and pork, and sauté until browned. Add the tomatoes and the reserved liquid from the chilies, and bring to a boil. Reduce the heat, add the bay leaves, and let simmer, uncovered, for 1 hour.

Meanwhile, place the chilies, cumin seed, garlic, oregano, paprika, chili powder, and sugar in a food processor or blender and purée. Add a little water if necessary. Stir the purée into the meat mixture and let simmer another 30 minutes. Season with salt and pepper to taste and serve immediately.

Makes 8 servings

Food is placed on thermal blankets, which serve as moisture-resistant tablecloths.

IRISH SODA BREAD

2	cups flour
2	teaspoons baking soda
2	teaspoons baking powder
½	teaspoon salt
4	tablespoons sugar
3	tablespoons sweet butter, softened
1	cup buttermilk
½	cup currants or raisins
2	tablespoons caraway seeds

Preheat oven to 375 degrees.

In a large mixing bowl or food processor, combine flour, baking soda, baking powder, salt, and 3 tablespoons of the sugar. Add butter and cut it into dry ingredients with a fork, pastry blender, or with on/off motions of the processor until mixture resembles coarse meal.

Add buttermilk, currants, and caraway seeds and mix well until all ingredients are moistened. Form into a ball and knead on a lightly floured surface for about 1 minute. Reshape into a ball and flatten slightly to form a round, rather flat loaf about 8 inches in diameter. Using a floured knife, cut a large, deep "X" in the top of dough, sprinkle with remaining tablespoon sugar, and place on an ungreased baking sheet. Bake in the center of the oven for 35 minutes, or until crust is nicely browned and bread sounds hollow when tapped lightly on the bottom. (The "X" may still appear slightly doughy, but the bread should be done inside.)

Makes one 8-inch round loaf

FRENCH ONION SAUTE
(Ham, Turkey, and Onion Sandwiches)

FOR EACH SANDWICH:

2 tablespoons vegetable oil
1 small onion, sliced
1 tomato, diced
1 hard Italian roll or a 6-inch piece of
   French bread cut in half horizontally
2 thin slices smoked turkey
2 thin slices smoked ham
2 thin slices imported Swiss cheese
   Dijon-style mustard

In a small skillet, heat oil, add onion and tomato, and sauté over medium heat until onion softens and excess moisture from tomato evaporates.

On one half of roll, stack ingredients in the following order: turkey slices, onion and tomato, ham slices, and cheese slices.

If desired, place under a hot broiler until cheese melts. Top with other half of roll and serve with mustard.

INDIAN PUDDING

4 cups milk
⅔ cup dark molasses
½ cup maple syrup
⅔ cup yellow corn meal
⅓ cup sugar
1 teaspoon salt
¾ teaspoon ground cinnamon
¾ teaspoon ground nutmeg
4 tablespoons butter, softened

Preheat oven to 225 degrees.

Combine 3 cups of the milk, the molasses, and syrup in the top half of a large double boiler and heat directly over medium-low heat to just below boiling; do not allow to boil. Remove from heat, stir in corn meal, sugar, salt, cinnamon, and nutmeg and place over simmering water. Stir in butter and cook, stirring, until thick.

Turn into a well-greased, 2-quart casserole. Pour remaining cup of milk over pudding—do not stir—and bake in the center of the oven for 6 hours. Serve warm with ice cream or whipped cream if desired.

Makes 6 to 8 servings

CHOCOLATE CHEESECAKE

CRUST:

1 8½-ounce package chocolate wafers
½ cup butter, melted
¼ teaspoon ground cinnamon

CAKE:

12 ounces semisweet chocolate
3 tablespoons butter
3 8-ounce packages cream cheese, softened
2 teaspoons vanilla extract
1½ cups heavy cream
1 cup granulated sugar
4 eggs, beaten

3 tablespoons cocoa powder, sifted

TO SERVE:

   Powdered sugar
   Fresh strawberries, hulled and dipped in
      melted chocolate (optional)

Preheat oven to 350 degrees.

Using a rolling pin, crush wafers between sheets of waxed paper. In a medium mixing bowl, combine crumbs with the ½ cup melted butter and cinnamon and blend well. Press mixture into a 9-inch cheesecake or springform pan.

In a small steel or glass bowl, melt chocolate with the 3 tablespoons butter in a 200 degree oven or over gently simmering water. Blend well, remove from the heat and let cool.

Beat cream cheese in a mixing bowl until fluffy. Beat in cooled chocolate mixture. Gradually stir in vanilla and cream and blend well. Mix granulated sugar, eggs, and cocoa together until creamy. Gradually stir the sugar mixture into the chocolate-cheese mixture and blend thoroughly.

Pour cake mixture into crust and bake in the center of the oven for 30 minutes. Turn off heat and let cake stand in oven with door slightly ajar for 30 minutes. Remove from oven and let cool at room temperature. Refrigerate overnight.

Just before serving, sprinkle with powdered sugar and decorate, if desired, with chocolate-dipped strawberries.

Makes 8 servings

HOT BUTTERED RUM

BATTER BASE:
2¼ cups firmly packed brown sugar
½ cup butter, softened
1 teaspoon ground cinnamon
Pinch ground cloves
Pinch ground nutmeg
2 tablespoons dark rum

TO SERVE:
2 cups dark rum
16 cinnamon sticks

In a large mixing bowl, combine sugar, butter, cinnamon, cloves, and nutmeg and sprinkle with the 2 tablespoons rum to soften mixture. Blend together and refrigerate until ready to prepare drinks.

To serve, place a heaping tablespoon of the batter base in each mug. Add an ounce of rum to each mug and pour in enough hot water to fill mug. Place a cinnamon stick in each mug as a swizzle stick and serve.

Makes 16 servings

SHRIMP GRILLED WITH HOT CHILI PEPPER RELISH

1¼   pounds jumbo shrimp (under 15 per pound)
½   cup hot chili pepper relish (purchased)
3   lemons, cut in wedges

Peel shrimp, leaving tails intact. Place them in a shallow baking dish, spread relish over them, and allow to marinate for at least 1 hour before grilling.

Thread a lemon wedge, 4 to 5 shrimp, and another lemon wedge on individual metal or bamboo skewers (see note). Turn skewers in relish to coat well.

Place skewers on a grill about 4 to 6 inches from hot coals and grill for about 3 minutes, turning once, and basting once or twice with the relish marinade.

Makes 4 servings

Note: To prevent bamboo skewers from burning over hot coals, soak them in water for an hour before grilling.

GRILLED ESCARGOTS

½   cup butter, softened
1   clove garlic, minced
2   teaspoons minced chives
14   snail shells
1   4½-ounce can large snails
14   1-ounce cubes Gruyère cheese, or other hard melting cheese such as Swiss or white Cheddar

In a small mixing bowl, combine butter, garlic, and chives and blend thoroughly.

Follow package directions for preparing snail shells. Stuff one snail snugly into each shell. Using a small butter knife, press an equal portion of seasoned butter into each shell. Then press a cheese cube into opening of each shell.

Place shells, open ends up, on a grill about 4 to 6 inches from hot coals and grill for 5 to 8 minutes, or until cheese melts and butter is bubbling.

Makes 4 servings

SEA SCALLOPS GRILLED WITH LIME BUTTER

½   cup butter, melted
     Grated zest of 1 lime
2   tablespoons fresh lime juice
1   pound large sea scallops (about 12)
2   to 3 limes, thinly sliced

Combine butter, lime zest, and lime juice in a small bowl.

Thread scallops and lime pieces onto 4 bamboo skewers (see note above), alternating 3 scallops with 2 lime pieces per skewer.

Place skewers on a grill about 4 to 6 inches from hot coals, brush with lime butter, and grill for 2 to 3 minutes, turning and basting often with lime butter.

Makes 4 servings

An open-hearth feast ready for the grill.

The pleasures of a New England ski weekend: fresh snow and fresh lobsters.

LOBSTERS GRILLED WITH LEMON BUTTER

¾ cup butter, melted
Juice and grated zest of 1 lemon
¼ teaspoon cayenne pepper
4 1-pound lobsters

Combine butter, lemon juice, zest, and cayenne in a small bowl.

Split each lobster cleanly down the center, brush with the lemon butter, and place on a grill about 4 to 6 inches from hot coals. Grill for 6 to 8 minutes, turning frequently and basting with remaining lemon butter.

Makes 4 servings

Marinated Skewered Beef served with Grilled Onions.

MARINATED SKEWERED BEEF

1¼   pounds top sirloin, cut into 1-inch pieces
½   cup soy sauce
1   1-inch piece fresh ginger root, peeled and grated
3   cloves garlic, minced
1   tablespoon olive oil

Place beef in a shallow baking dish, add soy sauce, ginger, garlic, and oil and turn meat in mixture to coat. Let marinate, refrigerated, overnight.

Thread 3 cubes of marinated beef onto individual metal skewers and brush each with the marinade.

Place skewers on a grill about 4 inches from hot coals and grill, turning once, for about 3 minutes.

Makes 4 servings

SWEET POTATOES GRILLED WITH ORANGE BUTTER

½   cup butter, melted
    Juice and grated zest of 1 orange
4   medium sweet potatoes, unpeeled

Combine butter, orange juice, and zest in a small bowl.

Place potatoes in a large saucepan of rapidly boiling water and boil for 20 to 25 minutes, or until fork tender, but not mushy.

Drain potatoes and place them (still unpeeled) on a grill about 4 to 6 inches from hot coals, brush with orange butter, and grill, turning and basting frequently with remaining orange butter, for about 20 to 25 minutes, or until skin is dark brown and glazed.

Makes 4 servings

Raclette cheese, melted and hot on a soapstone slab, for eating with bread and fruit.

MELTED RACLETTE CHEESE WITH PEARS, APPLES, AND FRENCH BREAD

1   pound raclette cheese (see note)
1   loaf French bread, sliced
2   pears, sliced into thin wedges
2   apples, sliced into thin wedges

Place cheese on a stone slab next to the fire and allow to soften and melt.

As cheese melts, let guests scrape melted portion off with a knife and spread onto bread, pear, and apple slices.

Makes 4 servings

Note: Raclette is a hard-rind Swiss cheese that melts slowly and evenly when exposed to direct heat.

GRILLED SHIITAKE MUSHROOMS, CUCUMBER, AND RED ONION

HERB BUTTER:

½   cup sweet butter, melted
3   to 4 sprigs fresh thyme or dill
¼   teaspoon freshly ground black pepper

8   whole fresh shiitake mushrooms or 8 whole dried, soaked in warm water and squeezed dry
1   cucumber, peeled and sliced into 2-inch pieces
1   large red onion, quartered

Combine the ingredients for the herb butter in a small saucepan and keep warm.

Thread the mushrooms, cucumber segments, and onion quarters onto separate bamboo skewers (see note on page 118). Place the skewers on a

Grilled Shiitake Mushrooms.

grill 4 to 6 inches from hot coals, baste generously with the herb butter, and grill for 5 to 8 minutes, turning and basting frequently.

Makes 4 servings

HOT SPICED WINE

1   bottle Burgundy wine
2   tablespoons sugar
3   whole cloves
1   2-inch piece cinnamon stick
¼   teaspoon ground allspice
    Dash Angostura bitters

In a large saucepan, combine all ingredients and warm over moderately low heat until hot. Do not allow to boil. To serve, ladle from a decorative heated crock or a copper kettle.

Makes 8 servings

Hot Spiced Wine and hot cider.

MOONLIGHT AND MARIACHIS

MEXICAN BUFFET

PICO DE GALLO
(FRESH TOMATO AND JALAPENO SAUCE)

MIXIOTES DE CAMARONES EN PEPIAN VERDE
(SHRIMP IN TOMATILLO AND PUMPKIN
SEED SAUCE)

RAJAS CON CREMA (CHILI STRIPS WITH
MOZZARELLA AND CREAM)

MANCHAMANTELES (CHICKEN WITH FRUIT
AND ALMONDS IN TOMATO CHILI SAUCE)

COCHINITA PIBIL (PORK IN ORANGE
AND ANNATTO MARINADE)

FRESH MANGOES

There comes a time even in this age of deliberate casualness when food and drink alone are not enough to foster a party spirit. At these moments our love of dramatic spectacle converges with a passion for novelty; we seek out the extraordinary effect, to transform the usual circumstances of entertaining into a rare and memorable occasion.

Late July is a difficult time for stimulating the imagination. The welcome warmth of June has become habitual by now, and days spent fishing and picnicking, swimming and camping, melt together in a sort of lazy sameness. On this Saturday afternoon the sun is radiating heat waves that rise limply toward the sky as preparations are underway for a poolside party for fifty guests. The venue is a home set amid gardens and fruit orchards with a view of New York's Long Island Sound. Poolside gatherings are as common as fields of late-summer corn in this rural landscape and are a popular hot-weather diversion wherever a group of friends, good food and drink, and an obliging pool owner are found. For this occasion, however, water sports will serve only as an aside to the main attraction of the evening, a Mexican supper buffet, complete with the music, lighting, and riotous colors of this sun-drenched country, set against the proscenium of a summer night.

Shortly after twilight the first guests begin to arrive and are escorted to the backyard where a dozen small tables are grouped around the pool. Each table is draped with a black tablecloth set with an array of boldly colored Fiestaware. Bouquets of bright garden flowers—yellow marigolds, red nasturtiums, and daisies—enhance the vibrant scheme. The entire effect is softened by the warm glow of candles and kerosene lamps on the tables, and, in the surrounding garden, *luminarios*, decorative paper bags filled with sand and candles, twinkle.

As a mariachi band strikes the first chords of the evening, festivities begin with margaritas, served straight up or iced for the faint of heart, and fresh tostado chips with spicy jalapeño chili-laced Pico de Gallo for dipping. Smiling a warm greeting of welcome, Zarela Martinez, the chef for the event and owner of Cafe Marimba in New York, invites guests to the buffet table, which offers a trove of Mexican riches for sampling.

Manchamanteles, a traditional recipe from Oaxaca, offers a rich contrast of textures and flavors; lightly poached chicken is combined with dried fruits, then topped with almonds and a cinnamony sweet-sour tomato sauce, and garnished with a border of sweet potatoes and bananas. "In Mexico people also eat with their eyes, and I plan my menu with color in mind," Zarela remarks. True to her intent, the startling hues of an Aztec palette

Vivid Fiestaware, centerpieces of marigolds, zinnias, and nasturtiums, and votive candles create a playful mood for the Mexican buffet.

A mariachi guitarist serenades with songs of love.

are in abundant display, such as in the dark sienna tint of Cochinita Pibil (a Yucatan entrée of pork in orange marinade). Throughout the meal, pitchers of fruity red and white sangria and icy Mexican beer provide refreshing coolers.

"People always associate Mexican food with a party," Zarela remarks. "It is fare for celebrating, for enjoying with close friends; hospitality is at the core of my culture." Mastery of the cuisine began with her mother, a well-known Mexican cook, from whom Zarela learned the exquisite regional specialties of her country, dishes, she explains, that are found only in the home in Mexico, not in any restaurant kitchen.

Zarela left her native state of Sonora and moved to Guadalajara as a university student. In this city famed for its excellent cuisine, she acquired further expertise from the cooks who worked in the boardinghouses she lived in, learning how to cook with banana and avocado leaves, pumpkin seeds, and other exotic ingredients such as the corn fungus *huitlacoche*, and to prepare the favorite Guadalajaran combinations of meat or poultry with fruit.

For Americans who know mostly the cowboy or border food of the North, such as mixed plate specials of tacos and refried beans, this buffet is a revelation of the complex flavors and tastes of Zarela's native specialties. "In our authentic cuisine, hot is but one accent among many sensations and flavors." Zarela explains that it is customary practice in her country to have on the table several sauces of varying degrees of spiciness, from mild to fiery. It is the diner's option to season according to personal preference.

To maximize flavor and freshness, everything for this party was prepared on the day of the event by Zarela and her staff. In planning an at-home version of this Mexican buffet, begin with a timetable to establish the sequence of preparation. Such items as the Mixiotes (shrimp with pumpkin seed sauce) can be assembled early in the day and refrigerated until final cooking and serving. To minimize last-minute work, fruits and vegetables should be washed and chopped in advance, then stored in plastic bags and kept chilled. Select and arrange the serving platters beforehand to determine how much table surface will be needed to accommodate all of

Reflections of a party: guests gather by the pool as festivities begin.

the items. In choosing platters and serving dishes, bear in mind the colors and shapes of these unusual foods. If guests are to help themselves, place the dinner plates and eating utensils on a separate surface area adjacent to the buffet (a small covered card table is a good choice).

After the copious feast, Zarela passes through the crowd with plates of fresh mango for dessert, an appropriately light and refreshing finale. In the darkening night, the waters of the swimming pool catch images of candlelight and swirls of bright colors from wide-skirted dresses as the mariachi band sings late into the night.

Overleaf: Appetizers include crisp fried squid and a variety of sauces with tortilla chips.

Kerosene lamps and candles softly illuminate the table.

PICO DE GALLO
(Fresh Tomato and Jalapeño Sauce)

2   large ripe tomatoes, finely chopped
1   fresh jalapeño chili, finely chopped
¼   cup finely chopped scallions (white and
      tender green part)
¼   cup finely chopped cilantro leaves
1   clove garlic, finely chopped
    Juice of 1 fresh lime
1   teaspoon dried oregano
½   cup water
    Salt

In a medium mixing bowl, combine all ingredients and stir to blend well. Refrigerate until serving. Serve with fresh grilled meat, burritos, tostadas, poached chicken, or simply as a dipping sauce for freshly made tortilla chips.

Note: For maximum flavor, do not prepare this sauce more than 1 hour ahead of serving time.

MIXIOTES DE CAMARONES EN PEPIAN VERDE
(Shrimp in Tomatillo and Pumpkin Seed Sauce)

3   tablespoons sweet butter
2   pounds medium shrimp, peeled and de-
      veined
1   tablespoon fresh lemon juice
    Salt
2   cups pepian verde sauce (recipe follows)
6   10-inch squares aluminum foil or parch-
      ment paper

Prepare pepian verde sauce.
Preheat oven to 400 degrees.
Heat butter in a large skillet. Add shrimp and

sauté over medium heat, part at a time, if necessary, for about 2 minutes, until barely pink. Sprinkle with lemon juice and season lightly with salt. Add pepian verde sauce and toss to coat shrimp thoroughly.

Spread foil or parchment out on a flat surface and divide shrimp evenly among the 6 squares. Fold each square over and crimp edges to form a packet. Place packets on a baking sheet in the oven and bake for 5 minutes. Serve immediately.

Makes 6 servings

Pepian Verde Sauce
(Tomatillo and Pumpkin Seed Sauce)

1   pound fresh tomatillos or one 10-ounce
      can (see note)
      Salt
2   fresh jalapeño chilies, cored, or 2 canned
      jalapeños (not pickled), drained
1   cup fresh cilantro leaves, stems removed
1   teaspoon minced garlic
1   large onion, finely chopped
2   tablespoons sweet butter
2   tablespoons vegetable oil
1   cup peeled pumpkin seeds
1   cup chicken stock
2   tablespoons lard (see note)
      Freshly ground black pepper

Peel off paper-like outer skin from fresh tomatillos and rinse. Cook in a saucepan of 2 cups boiling salted water for about 10 minutes. (If using canned, the tomatillos don't need to be boiled; drain the tomatillos, reserving liquid.) Drain, reserving cooking water. Place tomatillos, chilies, cilantro, garlic, onion, and ½ cup of the cooking water or liquid from canned tomatillos in an electric blender and process until smooth.

Transfer to a mixing bowl and set aside.

Melt the butter and vegetable oil in a heavy skillet, add pumpkin seeds and sauté over low heat, stirring constantly to prevent seeds from scorching, until lightly browned. (Scorched seeds will make the sauce bitter.) Place seeds and chicken stock in electric blender, and process until smooth.

Melt lard in a large saucepan, add tomatillo sauce and pumpkin seed mixture and simmer, stirring, over medium heat for about 3 minutes. Cool and use with Mixiotes de Camarones. The sauce can also be served with cooked spare ribs or poached or sautéed chicken breasts or whole pieces.

Note: Tomatillos are not green tomatoes. They are related to the cape gooseberry and are distant cousins of the Chinese gooseberry, or kiwi.

Lard contributes a distinctive smoky flavor to many Mexican dishes as it does to Chinese food. Butter or other shortening should not be substituted.

RAJAS CON CREMA
(Chili Strips with Mozzarella and Cream)

6   fresh poblano chilies or long green
      California chilies, roasted, peeled, and
      seeded, or two 4-ounce cans whole green
      chilies, rinsed
2   tablespoons lard or vegetable oil
1   clove garlic, peeled but left whole
1   large onion, cut in half through root end
      and vertically sliced
1   pound mozzarella cheese, cut into 1-inch
      cubes
2   cups half-and-half

Pat chilies dry on paper towels and cut lengthwise into ⅛-inch wide strips.

Heat lard or oil in a large, heavy skillet, add

garlic and sauté over medium heat for several minutes, pressing garlic gently with the back of a spoon to release flavor. Remove and discard garlic. Add onion and sauté for 1 minute. Add chili strips and sauté 1 minute longer. Add cheese cubes and reduce heat to low. Pour in half-and-half and simmer just until cheese begins to melt; do not allow to boil or the sauce will curdle. Remove from heat immediately and serve hot with flour or corn tortillas.

Makes 8 servings

Note: This may be made in advance up to the point of adding the cheese and half-and-half.

Golden spokes of mango make a refreshing dessert.

MANCHAMANTELES
(Chicken with Fruit and Almonds in Tomato Chili Sauce)

1   onion, quartered plus 1 onion, chopped
9   cloves garlic, crushed
5   bay leaves
2   3½-pound frying chickens, cut into pieces
6   fresh New Mexican red or ancho chilies, cored and seeded
2   tablespoons lard or vegetable oil
2   28-ounce cans Italian plum tomatoes, juice reserved and tomatoes coarsely mashed
1   teaspoon dried Mexican oregano
1½   teaspoons ground canela or cinnamon
½   teaspoon ground cloves
1   teaspoon ground cumin
     Salt
     Freshly ground black pepper
½   cup dry sherry or dry red wine
2   tablespoons sugar
1   tablespoon vinegar
1   16-ounce can pineapple chunks, drained and juice reserved
3   tart cooking apples, cored and cut into 8 wedges
1   cup pitted prunes
½   cup golden raisins
6   dried peach halves, cut into 2 pieces
6   dried pear halves, cut into 2 pieces
10   dried apricots, halved
1   cup slivered blanched almonds

In a large saucepan or kettle, place the quartered onion, 3 of the garlic cloves, 4 of the bay leaves, and 8 cups water. Simmer over medium-low heat for 15 minutes. Add chicken pieces and poach over low heat for 10 minutes. Remove chicken and set aside to cool. Reserve the poaching liquid.

Place chilies in a saucepan of boiling water and boil for 5 minutes. Drain and place in a blender with ½ cup of the reserved poaching liquid, and remaining 6 cloves garlic and blend until puréed. Strain the mixture through a sieve, discarding the pulp. Set purée aside.

In a large skillet, heat the lard or oil, add the chopped onion and sauté over medium heat for 2 minutes until softened, stirring frequently. Add the tomatoes and their juice. Stir in oregano, canela, cloves, cumin, and the remaining bay leaf. Season to taste with salt and pepper and cook over medium heat for 3 minutes. Stir in the sherry, sugar, vinegar, and reserved pineapple juice. Simmer for 2 minutes longer. Stir in the pepper purée and simmer 1 minute longer. Let sauce cool.

Preheat the oven to 350 degrees.

Meanwhile, remove the skin and any fat from poached chicken breasts and place them in one layer in a 3- to 4-quart ovenproof casserole. Spread pineapple chunks, apple wedges, prunes, raisins, dried peach and pear pieces, apricot halves, and almonds over the chicken.

Pour part of the cooled chili and tomato sauce into the blender and blend until puréed. Purée remaining sauce in batches. Strain sauce through a sieve, discarding the pulp. Pour sauce over chicken and fruit. Bake for 30 to 40 minutes, until the chicken is cooked. Adjust seasoning if necessary and serve hot.

Makes 8 servings

COCHINITA PIBIL
(Pork in Orange and Annatto Marinade)

1   2-ounce jar annatto or achiote paste (see note)
1½ cups freshly squeezed orange juice
2   cloves garlic
2   tablespoons cider vinegar
2   teaspoons ground cumin
    Salt
    Freshly ground black pepper
1   2-pound pork butt or shoulder, cut into 2-inch squares
1   package fresh banana leaves or aluminum foil

A frosty fire—iced margaritas.

Preheat oven to 325 degrees.

In a small glass bowl, soak annatto in orange juice for 15 minutes, breaking up with a fork as it softens. Place annatto, orange juice, garlic, vinegar, and cumin in a food processor or electric blender and process until smooth. Season with salt and pepper and pour into a large, shallow glass baking dish.

Place pork in baking dish and turn to coat meat thoroughly in annatto marinade. Cover and let marinate, refrigerated, overnight or for at least 6 hours before assembling dish.

Line a large, ovenproof casserole with banana leaves, fanning overlapping leaves out from center and allowing them to hang over casserole edges about 6 inches. (If using foil, allow the same amount of overhang.) Pile pork and marinade into the casserole and fold leaves or foil over the top to cover completely. If using leaves, cover with a lid or foil. Bake for 2 hours or until pork is very tender.

Let cool. Remove pork and shred or cut into ¼-inch cubes. Pile into a serving dish and pass with soft or hard taco shells for guests to fill with the pork. Accompany with pico de gallo sauce or pepian verde sauce (see pages 132 and 133).

Makes 6 servings

Note: The marinated pork may also be piled onto individual banana leaves, folded into packets and baked on a baking sheet covered with foil for 10 minutes, or until heated through. Serve as an entrée with hot corn or flour tortillas and salsa.

Annatto seeds may be used, but they are very hard and require a marble mortar and pestle or a lava stone to grind. If using powdered annatto seeds, add extra orange juice, extra cumin, and about 1 teaspoon Mexican oregano.

THIS SPORTING LIFE

TAILGATE PICNICS

Bloody Mary Soup

Saucisson au Vin

Toasted Potato Skins

Chicken Tonnato

Vegetable Rape

Potato Pie

Pear Tart

Hot Mocha Mousse

Almond Meringue Kisses

Chili con Queso

Lobster Bisque

Marinated London Broil with
Bearnaise Sauce

Apple Crisp

Grilled Spicy Short Ribs

Garlic-Crumbed Chicken Drumsticks

Cabbage Slaw

Whether the big game is a pigskin match between two small-town high schools or an Ivy League play-off where the discreet colors of striped neckties speak more volubly of team preference than the showiest razzle-dazzle of a cheerleader routine, one thing is certain: given two football teams, one stadium, and any assortment of vehicles, there will be a tailgate picnic (probably several) going on in the parking lot.

Sedan or station wagon, European sports car or Detroit's finest, the surrounding action can be as lively as a skirmish at the 10-yard line when the cars line up and their passengers stake out spots for pregame picnicking. Gone are the days when a fairly simple snack or six-packs of beer and hero sandwiches would suffice as fortification for the rigors of spectating. Now, an increasing number of tailgate enthusiasts devise elaborate, alfresco banquets with innovative menus and carefully planned table settings. Meats grilled over charcoal barbecues, formal presentations of fish and poultry dishes surrounded by heirloom silver and linen, imported cheeses, and fine wines are just a few of the many items likely to appear at updated versions of this outdoor entertainment.

True to the carefree spirit of picnics in general, anything goes for a tailgate party. The more imaginative the menu the better for hungry guests waiting as car trunks are opened. However, there are a few general guidelines for planning these portable feasts. In determining the menu, look for recipes that can be prepared almost completely in advance, requiring little last-minute work at the picnic site. Breads and sandwiches should be presliced, and desserts preportioned to eliminate the difficult job of cutting when space and equipment are limited. If barbecuing is part of the plan, select accompaniments that can be made ahead and are ready for snacking while the fire is being tended. To embellish the scene, add a few handsome serving platters, fresh flowers, and a pretty, washable tablecloth (old quilts are excellent).

On a blustery Saturday in November, the forecast for snow has not deterred the tailgate activities of a determined hoard of fans camped near the Yale Bowl in New Haven, Connecticut. By late morning it is already difficult to find a parking space, but for one foursome of picnickers, the McDonnells and Corbys from nearby Greenwich, early arrival ensured a comfortable spot close to the stadium.

Carol McDonnell and Margit Corby are professional caterers and cooking instructors, and for today's intimate, just-among-ourselves gathering, they have shared cooking and table-setting responsibilities for a casually elegant picnic that was prepared entirely in

Getting down to basics in the trunk of a Rolls Royce: iced Champagne, caviar, and pistachio nuts for nibbling.

Fans toast the home team at pregame parties.

advance. The party begins as Margit and husband Tom spread a handsome white patchwork quilt on the grass. An inexpensive white linen coverlet reserved for picnics is smoothed on top of the quilt, and flowers, silver candelabra, and wicker baskets follow. Hot Bloody Mary Soup, generously spiked with vodka, is poured into mugs from wide-mouth thermoses as a starter for a menu of the caterers' favorite easy-to-eat picnic foods such as Kielbasa and Toasted Potato Skins. Carol likes to bring at least one fancy, unexpected food, and for this occasion that's Chicken Tonnato, accompanied by slices of Potato Pie and a colorful salad of crisp carrots, zucchini, and parsnips. Individual Almond Meringues, Pear Tart, and Hot Mocha Mousse complete the meal.

A Saab-length away a family version of the pigskin picnic is underway. Debbie and Patrick Donahue, owners of Rory's Restaurant in Darien, Connecticut, and their two small children are preparing a barbecue. The heady aroma of the first course, Lobster Bisque, perfumes the air as it warms slowly in a kettle over the hot coals, while Frank Sinatra croons from a portable cassette player. To facilitate their tailgate dining, the Donahues have improvised a small two-legged card table that can be hooked to the back of their hatchback. Covered with a stain-resistant cloth, this portable table is ready to be set with sturdy china and eating utensils. Chili Con Queso and nachos for dipping and munching are served on heavy earthenware platters. A green salad is dressed and tossed at the table to accompany the grilled entrée, juicy London Broil that has been marinated in herbs, mustard, and garlic and is served with a warm Béarnaise Sauce, spooned from a thermos.

Nearby, another barbecue, featuring Grilled Spicy Short Ribs cooked over a small hibachi, is a welcome sight to guests who park their cars close-by and stroll over to the Jeep Wagoneer where a larger version of the tailgate party is in progress. Susan Ward of Greenwich, Connecticut, has draped a low portable table with plaid cloths and set it with bright plastic plates to create an informal and relaxed mood as guests help themselves to traditional picnic foods: golden chicken drumsticks with a crisp, garlicy breading, cabbage salad with raisins and sour cream, and

Before kickoff there is wine and a picnic hamper filled with hearty fare.

mugs of icy cold beer. And if the members of this casually attired group were to listen carefully, they would hear the clink of crystal goblets raised in a toast, as the owners of a black Mercedes entertain guests in a formal style a few yards away. Roast quail, bottles of fine red Bordeaux, and a sumptuous fruit compote, all served on crystal plates against a white lace cloth, present a striking pan-orama of how really good the good life can be.

Whatever the circumstances, Champagne and caviar for two or a generation-spanning family event, the essence of tailgating is creative ingenuity. Design the occasion to suit a personal style; what feels right and comfortable for the hosts sets guests at ease whether the mood is black-tie formal or blue-jeans casual.

BLOODY MARY SOUP

4   to 5 large, fresh ripe tomatoes, or
      one 28-ounce can Italian plum tomatoes,
      coarsely chopped
2   large, fresh red peppers, cored, seeded,
      and coarsely chopped
2   to 3 ribs celery with top leaves
1   10½-ounce can beef consommé with gelatin
1   teaspoon sugar
½   lemon
      Dash Tabasco
      Salt
      Freshly ground black pepper
½   cup vodka

TO SERVE:
      Celery ribs or lemon curls

Combine tomatoes, peppers, celery, consommé, 1 cup water, sugar, and lemon in a large saucepan or Dutch oven. Place over medium heat and simmer for about 30 minutes, or until tomatoes and peppers are very soft. Add Tabasco and season to taste with salt and pepper.

Remove celery tops and lemon and process mixture in a food processor or blender. Press mixture through a sieve or food mill to remove remaining seeds and skins.

Soup may be served hot or cold. Return to saucepan to heat through; add vodka and serve hot with lemon curls. Or refrigerate until well chilled, stir in vodka, and serve in chilled mugs with a celery rib in each.

Makes 4 to 6 servings

Note: If serving chilled, season generously as chilling will dull flavoring. This soup freezes well; freeze without vodka. Let thaw, then stir in vodka just before serving.

SAUCISSON AU VIN

1   pound Kielbasa or other country-style
      garlic sausage, quartered lengthwise,
      then cut in 1-inch slices
1   to 2 cups white wine
1   teaspoon sugar
2   tablespoons Dijon-style mustard,
      or to taste
4   tablespoons chopped parsley

Place sausage in one layer in a large saucepan or Dutch oven. Add enough wine to partially cover sausage. Place over medium-high heat and boil rapidly until wine has almost completely evaporated and looks syrupy. Sprinkle sugar over, add mustard and parsley, and toss well. Serve hot or at room temperature with toothpicks.

Makes 6 to 8 appetizer servings

TOASTED POTATO SKINS

      Skins from 3 or 4 large baked potatoes
      (flesh reserved for Potato Pie—recipe
      on page 144)
6   tablespoons butter, softened
½   to ¾ cup grated Parmesan, Monterey Jack,
      or Cheddar, or a mixture of grated
      cheeses
      Pinch chili powder
      Salt
      Freshly ground black pepper

Preheat oven to 350 degrees.

Generously brush inside of skins with softened butter. Sprinkle each with grated cheese and season with chili powder, salt, and pepper. Cut each skin into thick slices with kitchen scissors. Place on a baking sheet and bake in the center of the oven for 10 minutes or until they are crisp outside and cheese is melted and bubbly.

Makes 6 servings

CHICKEN TONNATO

3 whole chicken breasts, skinned and boned
½ cup dry white wine
1 lemon, cut in half
1 rib celery, sliced
1 scallion, chopped

SAUCE:
1 egg
2 egg yolks
½ teaspoon salt
1 teaspoon dry mustard
   Juice of ½ lemon
2 cups olive oil, or mixture of olive oil and
   vegetable oil
   Freshly ground white or black pepper
1 7-ounce can tuna fish, drained
5 to 6 flat anchovy filets, drained

TO SERVE:
   Watercress sprigs
   Capers
   Lemon slices

Split chicken breasts in half and flatten gently with a wooden mallet. Place in a large, straight-sided skillet with the wine, lemon, celery, and scallion, and poach, covered, over medium-low heat for about 10 minutes, or until chicken is just cooked. Turn off heat and let chicken cool in poaching liquid.

Place egg, egg yolks, salt, and mustard in a food processor and process for 30 seconds. Add lemon juice and process another 30 seconds. With processor running, add oil in a slow, steady stream through feed tube and process until thoroughly incorporated. (Add more lemon juice and pepper if desired.) Add tuna and anchovies to the mayonnaise in processor and process until well blended and smooth.

Remove chicken breasts from poaching liquid and pat dry. If transporting to a picnic, wrap each breast in aluminum foil. Place sauce in a plastic container with a secure top. When ready to serve, unwrap chicken breasts, arrange on a large platter or individual plates, and pour tonnato sauce over each. Garnish with watercress, capers, and lemon slices.

Makes 6 servings

Note: A good, commercially made mayonnaise can be substituted for homemade in the sauce if desired.

VEGETABLE RAPE

VINAIGRETTE:
¼ cup raspberry or cider vinegar
⅛ teaspoon dry mustard
   Pinch sugar
   Salt
   Freshly ground white pepper
½ cup oil

SALAD:
6 to 8 medium carrots, peeled
1 to 2 medium zucchini, unpeeled
1 to 2 medium parsnips, peeled
2 to 4 tablespoons chopped parsley and/or
   chives

In a small mixing bowl, blend vinegar, mustard, and sugar and season to taste with salt and pepper. Gradually whisk in the oil. (Dressing should be tangy, but if it tastes too tart, add a little more oil.)

With a hand grater or in a food processor fitted with a grating blade, coarsely grate carrots, zucchini, and parsnips. Place grated vegetables in a large mixing bowl with parsley and/or chives and toss well. (If preparing in advance and transporting to picnic without dressing, add a few tablespoons of oil or just enough to coat and toss through vegetables to prevent them from drying and discoloring.)

Just before serving, add dressing and toss well.

Makes 6 to 8 servings

POTATO PIE

3   large baking potatoes (see note)
2   to 3 tablespoons fresh bread crumbs
¾   cup grated Parmesan
1   to 2 tablespoons chopped parsley
1   cup ricotta (or cottage cheese, pressed through a sieve)
¼   cup half-and-half or milk
2   eggs
1   to 2 tablespoons chopped chives

Preheat oven to 450 degrees.

Bake potatoes in the center of the oven for 1 to 1½ hours, or until very tender.

In a small bowl, combine bread crumbs, 3 tablespoons of the Parmesan, and parsley and mix together well. Sprinkle mixture over bottom and sides of a generously buttered 8- or 9-inch pie or quiche pan and shake out excess crumbs. Chill until ready to fill.

Remove potatoes from oven and reduce oven heat to 350 degrees. Cut potatoes in half lengthwise and scoop out flesh into a large mixing bowl. (Set skins aside for toasting; see recipe on page 142.) While potatoes are still hot, beat in ricotta and half-and-half and continue beating until smooth. Beat in eggs, one at a time. Add chives and ¼ cup of remaining Parmesan and blend well.

Turn mixture into the prepared pie pan, sprinkle with remaining Parmesan and bake in the center of the oven for 35 to 45 minutes, or until puffy and lightly browned. Serve warm or at room temperature.

Makes 6 servings

Note: If you're not planning to toast the potato skins and you're short of time, 2 cups of instant (or leftover) mashed potatoes can be substituted. The pie can be made the day ahead. Or, the filling can be prepared and refrigerated for a day, then baked just before serving time.

PEAR TART

1   recipe pâte brisée sucrée (see appendix)
2   cups dry white wine or water (or half wine, half water)
2   tablespoons fresh lemon juice
½   cup sugar
1   cinnamon stick
2   pounds ripe pears, peeled, cored, and halved

FRANGIPANE FILLING:
½   cup sweet butter, softened
½   cup sugar
2   large eggs
1   cup ground blanched almonds
2   tablespoons flour
1   to 2 tablespoons pear brandy or Kirsch (optional)

GLAZE:
½   cup apricot preserves
1   tablespoon sugar

On a lightly floured surface, roll out pâte brisée dough to a ¼- to ⅛-inch thick round about 11 inches in diameter. Press dough into a 10-inch tart pan with removable bottom. Crimp edges to make a decorative border; prick bottom and sides of pastry shell with a fork and refrigerate for at least 30 minutes, or overnight if possible.

In a large, straight-sided skillet, combine wine, lemon juice, sugar, and cinnamon stick. Arrange pear halves, cut-side down, in one layer in skillet and poach, covered, over medium-low heat for 10 to 15 minutes, or until tender. Turn off heat and let pears cool in poaching liquid.

In a medium mixing bowl, cream softened butter and sugar together. Add eggs, one at a time, beating well after each addition. Stir in almonds, flour, and brandy and beat until thoroughly blended.

Preheat oven to 425 degrees.

Line chilled pastry shell with aluminum foil

Silver candelabra and a white linen coverlet over a patchwork quilt enhance an elegant buffet that includes (clockwise): fall apples, Vegetable Rapé crunchy with carrots and zucchini, Chicken Tonnato, and an almond-filled Pear Tart.

and fill with pie weights or raw rice. Bake in the center of the oven for 15 minutes. Remove foil and pie weights and bake 10 minutes longer, or until golden brown. Let cool.

Reduce oven temperature to 350 degrees.

Remove pears from poaching liquid and drain on a rack over paper towels. Set one whole pear half aside for center of tart. Place remaining pears, cut-side down, on a cutting surface and slice crosswise into ¼- to ⅛-inch slices, being careful to keep each pear half together.

Spread frangipane cream evenly over bottom of cooled tart shell. Using a large spatula, carefully transfer sliced pear halves to tart, arrang-ing them around edge of tart and placing re-maining whole pear half in the center of the tart.

Bake in the center of the oven for 30 minutes, or until custard is set and golden brown. (If crust begins to color too quickly, cover loosely with aluminum foil and continue baking.)

In a small saucepan, combine apricot pre-serves and sugar and heat until preserves are melted and sugar dissolved. Brush glaze over top of pears. Remove tart from tart ring and serve.

Makes 8 to 10 servings

HOT MOCHA MOUSSE

½ tablespoon cornstarch
¼ cup unsweetened cocoa powder, preferably Dutch process cocoa
½ teaspoon instant espresso powder
½ cup sugar
2 cups milk, or 1 cup milk and 1 cup
   half-and-half
¼ cup dark rum or Cognac

In a medium saucepan, combine cornstarch and ¼ cold water and whisk until dissolved. Sift cocoa, espresso powder, and sugar into saucepan and beat to a smooth paste over low heat with a wire whisk.

Bring to a simmer, whisking constantly. Slowly whisk in milk or half-and-half and simmer, stirring, until mixture is thick, glossy, and smooth. Stir in rum or Cognac and serve immediately, or pour into a thermos to keep warm until serving.

Makes 6 demitasse servings

ALMOND MERINGUE KISSES

½ cup lightly toasted, slivered almonds
½ cup plus 2 tablespoons sugar
1 teaspoon cornstarch
2 egg whites at room temperature
   Salt
   Pinch cream of tartar
½ teaspoon vanilla extract

Preheat oven to 200 degrees or lowest oven setting possible.

Combine almonds, 2 tablespoons sugar, and cornstarch in a food processor and process until finely ground but not yet powder.

In a small mixing bowl, beat egg whites until frothy. Add salt and cream of tartar and beat until stiff. Gradually sprinkle in ½ cup sugar, beating well. Add vanilla and beat for several minutes until very stiff and shiny. Gently fold in almond mixture.

Pipe mixture from a pastry bag fitted with a star tip or drop from a spoon to form meringue kisses about 2½ inches in diameter onto a baking sheet lined with parchment paper.

Bake in the center of the oven for about an hour, or until meringue is very dry.

Makes about 2 dozen 2½-inch meringue kisses

CHILI CON QUESO

5 cups grated Velveeta cheese
2 cups grated mild Cheddar
1 cup chopped onion
1 cup chopped tomatoes
4 jalapeño chilies, minced
2½ tablespoons chili sauce

Melt Velveeta and Cheddar together in the top of a double boiler. Add onion, tomatoes, and chilies, and simmer for 15 minutes. Stir in chili sauce and continue to heat over hot water until thick and smooth. Serve hot with nacho chips.

Makes 1 quart

LOBSTER BISQUE

1 1½-pound live lobster, or about 1 cup cooked, diced lobster meat
2 bay leaves
2 to 4 sprigs fresh thyme, or 1 teaspoon dried
1 sprig parsley
1 clove garlic
½ medium onion, plus 1 medium onion, minced
Salt
Freshly ground black pepper
5 tablespoons sweet butter
1 carrot, minced
½ cup white wine
3 cups chicken stock
¼ cup flour
1 cup milk
¼ cup dry sherry

Drop live lobster into a large pot of boiling water seasoned with 1 bay leaf, 1 sprig fresh thyme or ½ teaspoon dried thyme, 1 sprig parsley, 1 clove garlic, ½ onion, salt, and pepper and simmer gently for about 5 minutes. Drain immediately. When cool enough to handle, remove meat from shell and chop coarsely.

In a large saucepan, melt 3 tablespoons of the butter over medium-high heat. Add minced onion and carrot and sauté, stirring, until softened, about 5 minutes. (Do not allow vegetables to brown.) Stir in white wine, add lobster meat, and bring to a boil. Stir in chicken stock, remaining bay leaf and thyme, and allow to return to a boil. Reduce heat to medium-low and let simmer for about 15 minutes.

Meanwhile, melt remaining 2 tablespoons butter in another saucepan. Stir in flour and cook, stirring, over low heat for about 5 minutes. In a separate small saucepan, bring milk just to boiling point. Remove flour and butter mixture from heat, pour hot milk into it all at once, stirring constantly until well blended. Place over low heat and simmer, stirring, until very thick and smooth.

Pour white sauce into lobster/stock mixture, stirring vigorously until smooth, and simmer for another 15 minutes. Remove bay leaf (and thyme sprigs if using fresh). Stir in sherry and season with salt and pepper to taste. Serve hot.

Makes 4 servings

Spicy Chili Con Queso and nacho chips whet appetites.

MARINATED LONDON BROIL WITH BEARNAISE SAUCE

2½ pounds London broil
2 cups Rory's marinade (recipe follows)
1½ cups Béarnaise sauce (recipe follows)

Place London broil in a shallow baking dish, pour marinade over it, cover and refrigerate overnight, turning once or twice.

Remove meat from marinade and place over hot coals or under a hot broiler. Grill or broil to desired doneness, turning once, about 7 to 8 minutes per side for rare. Slice and serve with Béarnaise sauce.

Makes 4 to 6 servings

Rory's Marinade

⅓ cup vinegar
1 teaspoon dried oregano
1 teaspoon dried basil
1 bay leaf
1 teaspoon dried sage
1 teaspoon dried thyme
1 teaspoon dried rosemary
1 tablespoon Dijon-style mustard
1 teaspoon Tabasco sauce
1 teaspoon minced garlic
½ onion, minced
1 egg yolk
1 cup vegetable oil
Salt
Freshly ground black pepper

In a small mixing bowl, combine vinegar, oregano, basil, bay leaf, sage, thyme, rosemary, mustard, Tabasco sauce, garlic, and onion and blend well. Beat in the egg yolk. Add oil, a few drops at a time, beating after each addition until thick and smooth. Season with salt and pepper and blend well.

Makes about 2 cups

Béarnaise Sauce

1 shallot, minced, or 2 scallions (white and tender green part), minced
2 teaspoons dried tarragon
2 tablespoons wine vinegar
2 tablespoons white wine
3 egg yolks
1 cup plus 2 tablespoons sweet butter, melted
1 teaspoon fresh lemon juice
Dash Tabasco
Dash Worcestershire sauce
Salt
Freshly ground black pepper

In a small saucepan, combine shallot, tarragon, vinegar, and wine and bring to a boil. Reduce heat to medium and simmer until almost all liquid has evaporated. Set aside.

Place egg yolks in a metal mixing bowl over a pan of simmering water and whisk until thickened. Add melted butter a drop or two at a time, whisking constantly after each addition until all butter is incorporated. (If mixture becomes too thick, stir in a drop or two of water to thin.)

Remove from the heat and season with lemon juice, Tabasco, Worcestershire, salt, and pepper.

Stir in tarragon/shallot mixture. Taste and correct seasoning if necessary.

Makes about 1½ cups

Note: This sauce can be held briefly in the top half of a double boiler over hot water. Stir occasionally.

APPLE CRISP

8   tart apples, peeled, cored, and sliced
¼   cup granulated sugar
1   tablespoon lemon juice

TOPPING:
¼   cup granulated sugar
¼   cup firmly packed brown sugar
¾   cup flour
1   teaspoon ground cinnamon
¼   teaspoon salt
5   tablespoons cold sweet butter, cut into pieces

Preheat oven to 350 degrees.

Place apples in a large mixing bowl, add granulated sugar and lemon juice, and toss together well.

In a separate mixing bowl, combine granulated and brown sugars, flour, cinnamon, and salt. Add butter and cut into dry ingredients with a fork or a pastry blender until mixture resembles coarse crumbs.

Turn apple slices into a lightly greased, 10-inch pie pan. Sprinkle topping mixture evenly over apples and bake in the center of the oven for about 45 minutes, or until browned and bubbling.

Serve warm with a scoop of vanilla ice cream.

Makes 8 servings

GRILLED SPICY SHORT RIBS

2   28-ounce cans tomatoes
⅓   cup cider vinegar
1   small onion, minced
1   tablespoon honey
2   teaspoons dry mustard
2   tablespoons brown sugar
1   tablespoon Worcestershire sauce
1   lemon, sliced
    Hot Sichuan chili flakes
    Dash hot Chinese chili oil
4   pounds short ribs
    Salt
    Freshly ground black pepper

Drain tomatoes, reserving juice, and chop. In a medium saucepan, combine tomatoes and their juice, vinegar, onion, honey, mustard, brown sugar, Worcestershire, and lemon and season to taste with chili flakes and chili oil. Bring to a boil over medium-high heat, reduce heat and let simmer, stirring occasionally, for 30 minutes.

Preheat oven to 450 degrees.

Season the ribs with salt and pepper and place on a baking sheet lined with aluminum foil. Bake in the center of the oven for 8 to 10 minutes, turning to brown on all sides. Remove from the oven and let cool. Place ribs in a shallow baking dish, pour sauce over them, cover, and let marinate overnight in the refrigerator.

Place ribs on a grill about 4 inches from hot coals and grill, turning and basting frequently with the sauce, for 25 to 35 minutes, or until medium-rare.

Makes 4 servings

GARLIC-CRUMBED CHICKEN DRUMSTICKS

2 tablespoons fresh lemon juice
2 cloves garlic, minced
¼ teaspoon Tabasco
½ cup plain yogurt
Salt
Cayenne pepper
12 chicken drumsticks, skinned
1 cup finely crushed soda crackers
1 tablespoon dried oregano
1 teaspoon dry mustard
1 teaspoon paprika
4 tablespoons butter, melted

In a shallow baking dish large enough to hold all the drumsticks, combine lemon juice, garlic, Tabasco, and yogurt and season with salt and cayenne. Place drumsticks in the dish, turn to coat with the yogurt mixture, cover, and let marinate for at least 3 hours.

Preheat oven to 375 degrees.

Combine the cracker crumbs, oregano, mustard, and paprika in a large, shallow dish and season with salt and cayenne. Roll the marinated drumsticks in the crumbs to coat well and place them on a greased baking sheet lined with aluminum foil. Brush drumsticks all over with melted butter. Bake in the center of the oven, turning occasionally, for 45 minutes, or until tender and golden brown. Serve hot or at room temperature.

Makes 4 to 6 servings

CABBAGE SLAW

1 small head green cabbage, shredded
1 cup raisins
½ cup toasted, slivered almonds
¾ cup sour cream
Salt
Freshly ground black pepper

Combine the cabbage, raisins, and almonds in a large mixing bowl. Add the sour cream and toss well, adding more sour cream if slaw seems too dry. Season with salt and pepper and toss again. Cover and chill until ready to serve.

Makes about 8 servings

A bright plaid tablecloth and plastic plates set a casual mood for enjoying Garlic-Crumbed Chicken Drumsticks served from a wicker basket and crispy Cabbage Slaw. On the grill, short ribs basted with a spicy marinade turn deep brown and tender.

PHEASANTS, DOGS, AND OLD ROSES

HUNTERS' DINNER

Oysters on the Half Shell

Hazelnut Pasta with Shiitake Mushrooms

Pheasant Breasts in Champagne Sauce

Steamed Spinach with Balsamic Butter

Watercress Salad

Raspberry Layer Pudding

To the unitiated, the sport of hunting is an enigma, confounding and allowing few comparisons with other leisurely pursuits. Stalking partridge or quail in a field of harsh, sun-leathered grass, or crouching at the edge of a soggy marsh in wait for duck or pheasant to appear is one aspect of it. So too is "being outdoors in a woods with the sun and trees, with my dogs and with people I love," as one seasoned marksman explains. Simply put, the world is divided into those who do and those who don't. For the participants, it is this unparalleled combination of active thrill and meditative serenity that is irresistible.

And on this first Saturday in October a gathering of friends has assembled, as they have for the past several years, at the East Mountain Preserves in Dover Plains, New York. Set amid the meandering hills and deep blue rivers of the Upper Hudson Valley, the site is a game preserve abundantly stocked with pheasant, quail, and other game birds and offers facilities for both tower and field shooting. This morning, as the hunters arrive in cars and station wagons, they first unload several picnic hampers and head for a small gunners' cabin heated by a wood-burning stove. Equipped with refrigerator, tables, and chairs, it will be the cozy rendezvous spot for lunch later in the day. As soon as food and provisions are unpacked, the party is ready to begin the hunt.

The first half of the day is to be devoted to tower shooting. Armed with shotguns, the hunters disperse at 50-yard intervals in a rough circle surrounding a tower. On signal, pheasants are released from the top of the tower and as a bird flies within range the hunters are permitted two shots. A group of good marksmen will yield about 50 percent of the 100 to 200 birds let loose during a morning shooting period. Today's tally is 75 pheasant.

After three hours of shooting, a sudden silence falls—the tower hunt is at an end. Soon the hunters pack up and return to the cabin for lunch. To allow plenty of time for the remainder of the day's activities, this meal is customarily a short, casual break. Set in the manner of a seventeenth-century Dutch still life, the table presents a handsome offering of bread, cheese, fruit, and wine. Arranged within a hand-hewn wooden trough are grapes, apples, and several varieties of pears. Nearby is a round of Stilton cheese, crumbly and ripe with age. There is also a smooth-textured duck liver pâté, seasoned with Cognac, herbs, and heavy cream and served from an earthenware terrine. Bottles of red wine are poured and the group toasts the morning's sharpest shooter.

In less than an hour hunters head off for the field shoot accompanied by breeders and their pack of superbly trained dogs—Brittany spaniels and wire- and short-haired pointers. The group treks over flat fields and rocky

The smoky gray hills of the Upper Hudson Valley provide a serene prospect for the field shoot.

hills, passing a cedar swamp enclosed in the 600 acres of the game preserve. Soon a pointer quivers with alertness and a hunter fires; the first pheasant is downed with a single shot.

As more birds are felled, they are quickly retrieved by the dogs, which return the prizes to their breeders. Immediately, the birds are field-dressed and strung onto strap carriers, then placed under the shade of a tree. At the end of the day the bounty is brought back to the cabin where it is divided equally among the hunters. On this occasion, including morning and afternoon hunts, there are eight birds per hunter, and a dozen couples will soon share their good fortune with a celebration.

This evening, as in years past, a traditional

Pointer Diana returns with her quarry.

formal dinner party will be held at an obliging hunter's country home. To honor the
hunt in a grand manner there will be excellent table service, fine wines, and a feast of
fresh pheasant caught on the preserve a few
days earlier and prepared for the occasion
by Sara Foster, a talented young chef from
Greenwich, Connecticut.

While tradition is the essence of game bird
cookery, controversy is its salt, and as the host
and a few experienced hunter/cooks work
with Sara in the kitchen, conversation turns
to the many diverse opinions concerning the
three stages involved in wild poultry preparation: hanging, marinating, and cooking. A
hunter with a bag of freshly killed birds has
two choices—either to cook them immediately or preserve them for later use. The latter can be done by aging or freezing or a
combination of both methods. When it's to

be served fresh, the bird should be dressed,
cleaned, washed, then used within a matter
of hours. It can also be wrapped carefully in
airtight freezer bags and frozen at this point.
When properly cooked the meat is delicate
in flavor with a slightly resilient texture.

Hanging the birds is an aging procedure
employed to develop the full-bodied, winy
intensity that distinguishes game from domes-
ticated fowl. It also imparts tenderness and a
meltingly smooth texture. Several different
methods are used for hanging, but the one
most favored by this group of hunters is the
following: after cleaning, dry the birds completely with paper towels to remove all
moisture, then hang in a dry refrigerator, a
cool dry cellar, or, in cool weather, outdoors,
for three to five days. The aged poultry is
then ready to use, or it can be frozen for fu-
ture preparation.

After hanging, the next stage is marinating,
and an important rule to follow is to select
seasonings that will enhance rather than over-
whelm the natural flavors of the game. Begin
with an acid, such as lemon juice, wine, or
vinegar, to break down muscle tissue and
tenderize. Always marinate the meat in a non-
metal container, such as glass or pottery, to
avoid discoloration and a metallic taste. Fresh
herbs and seasonings can enliven flavors; juniper berries, garlic, and shallots are classic
seasonings, and herbs such as rosemary,

The long, silent wait is the heart of a hunt.

A silken Duck Terrine for lunch.

thyme, and tarragon are excellent complements to game birds.

Since wild birds spend most of their lives actively hunting for food, they contain little subcutaneous fat. Consequently, the flesh is lean, somewhat sinewy in texture, and benefits from additional fat during cooking and saucing to prevent dry, unappetizing meat. For pheasant and other game birds, butter, salt pork, or light and fruity olive oils are good for cooking purposes; butter and heavy cream make flavorful binding agents to blend with pan juices and seasonings in preparing sauces for the poultry.

Leaving Sara to complete her last-minute preparations, the crew retires to dress for dinner. Promptly at eight o'clock a dozen formally attired couples arrive at the home of their hosts, William and Barbara Gray Schaefer Jr. Soon the party moves to the dining room where the buffet table is elegantly set for the occasion. Lit by the glimmer of soft candlelight, fine heirloom silver and antique English dinner plates are set on a nineteenth-century chintz coverlet, as brilliantly patterned as a peacock's tail spread. A dramatic bouquet of snapdragons, Queen Anne's lace, stock, and heather is placed at one end of the table and a finely carved duck decoy is poised at the opposite end. Rough stone walls and wood-beamed ceilings add to the enchantment of this rustic retreat.

Using the classic rules of game cookery as a foundation, the chef offers an innovative menu. Tonight's first course, served on French porcelain *barbotines* (oyster plates), is briny fresh Oysters on the Half Shell, seasoned with soy sauce, brown sugar, and scallions. A sectioned sterling silver tray contains the entrée, pheasant breasts sautéed in butter until amber-gold and moistly tender, then served with a Champagne sauce. Arranged on either side are its accompaniments, steamed spinach flavored with balsamic vinegar and nutty strands of hazelnut pasta studded with fresh shiitake mushrooms. The pasta's earthy, toasted flavor is an excellent complement to the gaminess of the poultry. Curls of fresh watercress, ripe Bosc pear slices, and blue cheese make a refreshing salad course. Later on there will be Raspberry Layer Pudding, redolent with brandy and ripe berries and dark scarlet in hue, like the roses that brighten the dessert table.

Antique English dinner plates, French oyster plates, silver, and a handsome duck decoy accent the hunt dinner that includes: Oysters on the Half Shell, Pheasant Breasts in Champagne Sauce, Hazelnut Pasta, and Steamed Spinach with Balsamic Butter.

A mature, full-bodied red wine is a suitable accompaniment for the robust flavors of game; classic selections favored by experienced game cooks include fine old Bordeaux and Burgundies, Rhône wines such as Châteauneuf du Pape and Hermitage, and vintage California Cabernet Sauvignons. For this celebration the choice is a superb Bordeaux, Château Mouton-Rothschild (1970), admittedly a luxury, but the first hunt of the season comes only once a year and the game will never be so sweet as tonight.

OYSTERS ON THE HALF SHELL

3 dozen fresh oysters in the shells
3 tablespoons balsamic vinegar
1 tablespoon soy sauce
½ teaspoon brown sugar
¾ cup olive oil
6 scallions (green part only), thinly sliced

Shuck the oysters and place on the half shell on a platter or individual serving plates.

In a small mixing bowl, combine vinegar, soy sauce, sugar, and olive oil. Spoon mixture over each oyster. Sprinkle with scallions and serve.

Makes 6 servings

HAZELNUT PASTA WITH SHIITAKE MUSHROOMS

PASTA:
2 cups flour
1 tablespoon salt
1 tablespoon ground toasted hazelnuts
3 eggs plus 1 egg yolk
1 tablespoon hazelnut oil

SAUCE:
4 tablespoons butter
2 tablespoons hazelnut oil
½ pound fresh shiitake mushrooms, sliced
2 tablespoons ground toasted hazelnuts
¼ cup grated Parmesan cheese

In a food processor fitted with a metal blade, combine flour, salt, and hazelnuts and process for 1 to 2 minutes. Add eggs, yolk, and oil and continue to process until dough forms a ball. Remove dough and knead on a lightly floured surface for a few minutes. Wrap in plastic wrap and refrigerate for 1 to 2 hours.

Divide dough into 2 or 3 balls and roll out to about ¹⁄₁₆ inch thick with a pasta machine or by hand with a rolling pin. Roll up each sheet of pasta and cut into strips of desired width, ¼

inch for tagliatelle, ⅛ inch for taglierini. Toss pasta in corn meal to prevent sticking and hang to dry slightly. (Fresh pasta can be cooked after drying for several minutes, or can be hung on a drying rack for up to an hour. If making pasta more than an hour before cooking it, lay it between 2 cotton towels sprinkled lightly with flour or corn meal and keep like this for up to 12 hours. If making pasta 3 to 4 days ahead, let dry uncovered for 2 hours, then store in a plastic bag until ready to use.)

In a medium skillet, melt the butter in the oil. Add mushrooms and sauté over high heat for 1 to 2 minutes.

Meanwhile, drop the fresh pasta into a large pot of boiling water and cook until done; very fresh pasta (just made) requires only 15 seconds to 1 minute of cooking, depending on width. Pasta that has been dried and stored from 2 hours to 4 days needs from 1 to 3 minutes.

Drain pasta well, pour mushroom sauce over it, and toss with hazelnuts and cheese. Serve immediately.

Makes 6 servings

PHEASANT BREASTS IN CHAMPAGNE SAUCE

6 pheasant breasts
4 shallots, thinly sliced
2 cloves garlic, crushed
4 tablespoons juniper berries, crushed
   Salt
   Freshly ground black pepper
1 bottle Champagne
6 tablespoons clarified butter
10 tablespoons cold butter, cut into 10 pieces

Freshly-caught pheasant.

Place breasts, skin side up, in a large shallow baking dish. Sprinkle with shallots, garlic, juniper berries and season with salt and pepper. Reserving ½ cup of the Champagne for sauce, pour remaining Champagne over breasts. Cover with aluminum foil and let marinate, refrigerated, for 1 to 3 days.

In a large skillet, heat clarified butter over high heat. Add breasts (in two batches, if necessary), skin side down, and sauté for 2 to 3 minutes, or until golden brown. Reduce heat, cover and simmer for 4 to 5 minutes. Remove cover, increase heat to high, turn breasts, and sauté for 5 to 6 minutes longer, or until cooked through. Remove from pan and keep warm while making sauce.

Pour off butter from skillet, add reserved ½ cup of Champagne and boil over high heat until reduced to a glaze. Remove skillet from heat and add butter, 1 piece at a time, whisking thoroughly after each addition until all butter is incorporated. Season with salt and pepper to taste. Pour warm sauce over breasts and serve immediately.

Makes 6 servings

STEAMED SPINACH WITH BALSAMIC BUTTER

2 tablespoons balsamic vinegar
2 tablespoons red wine
2 pounds fresh spinach leaves, stems
      removed
½ cup cold butter, cut into 8 pieces
   Salt
   Freshly ground black pepper

In a small saucepan, combine vinegar and wine and simmer over medium-high heat until reduced by half.

Meanwhile, using only the water remaining on spinach after rinsing, steam leaves in a large saucepan over high heat until wilted, about 2 or 3 minutes.

Remove reduced vinegar/wine mixture from the heat and add butter, 1 piece at a time, whisking thoroughly after each addition until all butter is incorporated. Season with salt and pepper to taste.

Transfer spinach to a serving dish, add butter sauce, toss through, and serve hot.

Makes 6 servings

Overleaf: Lunch in the gunners' cabin amid mementos of hunts past.

WATERCRESS SALAD

2   tablespoons wine vinegar
     Juice of ½ lemon
¼   cup olive oil
¼   cup vegetable oil
2   tablespoons heavy cream
     Salt
     Freshly ground black pepper
2   bunches watercress, stems removed
½   cup crumbled blue cheese
2   Bosc pears, peeled and sliced into wedges

In a small mixing bowl, combine vinegar, lemon juice, olive oil, vegetable oil, and cream, season to taste with salt and pepper, and blend thoroughly with a whisk.

Place watercress, cheese, and pears in a salad bowl. Pour dressing over salad, toss thoroughly, and serve immediately.

Makes 6 servings

RASPBERRY LAYER PUDDING

DOUGH:
2   cups flour
2   teaspoons baking powder
¼   cup sugar
     Pinch salt
½   cup sweet butter, cut into pieces
2   eggs, beaten

FILLING:
1½   pints raspberries
     Sugar for sprinkling
½   cup brandy

SAUCE:
¼   pint raspberries
¼   cup Framboise, or other raspberry liqueur

In a large mixing bowl, combine flour, baking powder, sugar, and salt. Add butter and cut into the dry ingredients with a fork or pastry blender until mixture resembles coarse meal. Blend in the eggs and add just enough cold water to bring dough to a soft consistency (about 1 to 2 tablespoons).

On a lightly floured surface, roll out dough to about ⅛-inch thick and cut out progressively larger rounds—the first to fit the bottom of a round, 5-inch pudding mold, the following ½-inch larger, the next ½-inch larger, and so on.

Place the smallest round in the bottom of the well-greased pudding mold. Top with a layer of raspberries and sprinkle with sugar. Place the next largest layer of pastry dough on top, followed by a layer of raspberries and sugar. Continue in this manner until all raspberries are used, finishing with the last pastry round. Sprinkle with sugar and cover mold securely with aluminum foil.

Steam the pudding for 2½ to 3 hours on top of the stove by placing a trivet inside a large pot and pouring in water almost to the level of the trivet. Place the pudding container on it and cover. Bring the water to a boil, then reduce to a simmer. Occasionally check the water level and add more if it becomes too low. To test for doneness, gently press the top of the pudding with a finger; it should be resilient.

When cooked, remove the foil. Pierce pudding with a long, thin knife and pour brandy over it. Allow pudding to absorb brandy for 10 minutes before turning out.

Meanwhile, press raspberries through a fine sieve into a small saucepan. Add liqueur and warm over low heat until warm.

Invert mold and turn pudding out onto a serving plate. Sprinkle top with sugar and pour warm sauce over the top. Serve warm.

Makes 6 servings

Raspberry Layer Pudding and full-blown roses for the dessert table.

GIVING IN TO EXCESS

DESSERT PARTY

ALMOND CAKE

BLACK GRAPE TART WITH KIWI

FIGS STUFFED WITH RASPBERRIES

RASPBERRY CHOCOLATE CAKE

FROZEN MOCHA MOUSSE TART WITH
CHOCOLATE CURLS

FRUIT CORNUCOPIA

CASSIS SORBET

GOOSEBERRY BARQUETTES

MILLE ET UNE FEUILLES

ORANGE CURD TART

PITHIVIERS (ALMOND PUFF)

POACHED PEARS

SHELL-SHAPED DACQUOISE

RHUBARB SORBET

STRAWBERRY TART IN AN ALMOND NUT CRUST

PHYLLO TARTS

Of the many traditional culinary combinations, sweetly ripe raspberries showered with heavy cream is an acknowledged classic among desserts. But, to give hedonism its due—and who, among lovers of fine food, does not enjoy occasionally gilding the lily?—there are times when we crave more voluptuous pleasures, when nothing will do but to blanket the berries between layers of pastry and butter cream or maybe to purée them into a sauce dolloped over fat, green figs.

Autumn is the best of all seasons to experiment with confections and fine pastries, when the finest of fresh fruits beckon from every market—melons, peaches, tart red currants, and the first crisp apples. Color, texture, and flavor are prime and intense, whether the fruits are used singly or in appealing combinations—cool green slices of kiwi nestled against plump blackberries; firm-fleshed early pears poached in red wine; or sweet-tart currants made into an icy cassis sorbet.

A dessert party provides an excellent opportunity for the baking enthusiast both to experiment with a variety of pastry techniques and to entertain in a charmingly unconventional fashion. This is, however, an event that calls for careful planning, so before rushing off to the orchard or greengrocer for provisions, outline your strategy. For a party of eight to ten guests, plan on serving three to four different desserts; for larger groups, from twelve to twenty, serve six to eight choices. You might want to consider making the event a group effort by asking a few guests to contribute a selection.

When combining different items to create an interesting menu, there are several factors to keep in mind. There should be a good balance of flavors, from delicate to intense, and a variety of different fruits should be used, rather than repeating a single category such as berries. The textures of the offerings should also have diversity, from the smooth finesse of poached fruits to the delicate crispness of a meringue-based torte. Color is essential to an appealing presentation; the dessert table should present a spectrum from pastel shades to deep hues. For additional color plan on decorating the desserts and platters with fresh garden flowers.

It's important to estimate in advance how much time will be necessary for each recipe, which can be made either partially or entirely ahead, and which require last-minute work. Perishability of certain items should also be considered. If the party takes place outdoors, pay particular attention to foods that will melt or wilt, such as a sorbet or cut fruit. When serving these items either scoop individual portions into dessert goblets and chill until serving, or present half the amount in a large serving bowl and replenish as needed. Large single items such as cakes and tarts should be displayed in their entirety to preserve the beauty of their form. The best way to serve this type of menu is buffet-style, inviting

A winsome dessert harvest (clockwise from bottom left): Nectarine and Cherry Tart, Black Grape Tart with Kiwi, Raspberry Tart, Orange Curd Tart, Blackberry Tart, Gooseberry Barquettes, and (center) Strawberry Tarts in an Almond Nut Crust.

guests to serve themselves.

For Jane Stacey of Westport, Connecticut, inviting friends over to sample the superb results of her pastry-making wizardry is a favorite mode of entertaining. Invariably, the first cool day in September will draw this talented cook and caterer to her kitchen to begin whipping egg whites into a snowy drift of peaks for a meringue or to prepare a buttery puff pastry dough that will be used in any number of inventive creations. On this brilliantly sunny, crisp Sunday afternoon a dozen friends have gathered in the pleasant garden of her Colonial home. Amid colorful patches of autumn flowers—marigolds, asters, and chrysanthemums—a long, rectangular table is set with stacks of gold and white china and a glorious spread of desserts.

Magenta mounds of Cassis Sorbet.

Many of these items are based on classics of French pastry, varied here with innovative adaptations in shape and ingredient. The Dacquoise, three crisp layers of hazelnut-flavored meringue, sandwiched with a silken coffee butter cream filling, is one of several meringue-based tortes that have been popular in France since the reign of Louis XIV. Legend notes that Marie Antoinette would often enter the royal kitchens and whip up meringue concoctions for guests at the Trianon, her private little sanctuary behind Versailles.

A small town about fifty miles south of Paris gives its name to Pithiviers—another French pastry Jane has prepared for today's party. This regional specialty is traditionally composed of a smooth almond paste center baked in a puff pastry pillow scored on top in a pinwheel pattern and scalloped around the edges. For an easy and equally handsome alternative, Jane bundles a sheet of puff pastry around the filling, then ties it to resemble a fragile, golden purse.

Mille-et-Une Feuilles is an elaboration of a classic tart with countless delicate, flaky pastry sheets layered with fresh raspberries and pastry cream and dusted with powdered sugar. *Mille feuilles*, literally a thousand leaves, refers to the more than 700 layers of paper-thin pastry leaves created by the rolling and folding technique used to make puff pastry.

A simple-to-prepare country shortbread, fashioned into a cornucopia shape, makes a handsome—and edible—basket for fruits. A richer selection is the Chocolate Terrine, dense chocolate sponge cake layered with semisweet chocolate and Cognac mousse, glazed with a chocolate ganache, and decorated with chocolate curls.

For sipping with these winsome creations, Jane has on hand pitchers of iced tea and iced coffee and two chilled sweet wines, a German Auslese and a Sauternes. A sparkling wine such as Codorniu from Spain would also be a festive accompaniment. And for special occasions, of course, break out the Champagne.

Fresh raspberries crown a dense Chocolate Cake next to a compote of Rhubarb Sorbet.

Almond Cake, fragrant with orange flower water.

ALMOND CAKE

1 cup sweet butter, softened
⅔ cup sugar
8 ounces almond paste
3 eggs
¼ teaspoon orange flower water
¼ cup flour
⅓ teaspoon baking powder

GLAZE:
1 cup apricot preserves
1 tablespoon Grand Marnier

Preheat oven to 350 degrees.

In a large mixing bowl, cream butter, sugar, and almond paste together with an electric mixer until light and fluffy. Add eggs and flower water, and beat at high speed for 2 to 3 minutes. Sift in flour and baking powder and beat just until blended; do not overbeat.

Pour batter into a generously buttered and floured 4-cup ovenproof ring mold or other baking pan and bake in the center of the oven for 30 to 40 minutes, or until a toothpick inserted in center of cake comes out clean. Let cool in the pan for 15 minutes.

In a small saucepan, bring the apricot preserves to a boil. Strain through a fine sieve. Stir in Grand Marnier.

Turn cake out onto a plate; it should still be slightly warm. Brush about half of the glaze over top and sides of cake. Let cake absorb glaze for a few minutes, then brush on the remaining glaze.

Makes 8 to 10 servings

Note: This cake will keep for 5 days if wrapped tightly and stored in a cool place. It also freezes very well.

BLACK GRAPE TART WITH KIWI

1 recipe pâte brisée (see appendix)

PASTRY CREAM:
1 cup milk
½ cup heavy cream
3 tablespoons sugar
1 tablespoon flour
1 tablespoon cornstarch

1 egg
1 egg yolk
½ teaspoon vanilla extract
1 tablespoon sweet butter

TO ASSEMBLE:
2 pounds black grapes, preferably Emperor, halved and pitted

4 to 5 fresh ripe kiwis, peeled and cut into 6 lengthwise wedges

½ cup apple jelly

Prepare the pâte brisée dough, wrap in plastic wrap, and refrigerate for 20 to 30 minutes.

Meanwhile, prepare pastry cream. In a medium saucepan, combine milk, cream, and 2 tablespoons of the sugar and bring slowly to a boil. While milk heats, combine flour, cornstarch, and remaining tablespoon sugar in a mixing bowl. Add egg and egg yolk and beat with a wire whisk until smooth. When milk comes to a boil, remove from heat and gradually pour about half of it into egg mixture, whisking until smooth. Pour egg-milk mixture back into saucepan, place over low heat and warm, stirring constantly, until thickened and almost boiling. Remove from heat and stir in vanilla and butter. Transfer to a mixing bowl, cover surface of pastry cream with plastic wrap to prevent a skin from forming, and let cool. Chill well before assembling tart.

Preheat oven to 375 degrees.

On a lightly floured surface, roll chilled dough out to a ⅛-inch thick round, about 11 inches in diameter. Press into a 9- or 10-inch tart pan with a removable bottom. Refrigerate pastry shell for 10 minutes. Line shell with aluminum foil and fill with pie weights or dried beans to prevent pastry from puffing up and shrinking while baking. Bake in the center of oven for 15 to 20 minutes. Remove weights and foil and continue to bake shell until crust is golden brown and dry. Let cool.

To assemble tart, spread the chilled pastry cream over the bottom of cooled pastry shell. Starting at the edge and working toward the center, arrange grape halves as close together as possible in a spiral pattern. Arrange kiwi slices in the center of the tart in a petal-like formation.

In a small saucepan, warm jelly with 2 tablespoons of water, stirring constantly until mixture comes to a boil and begins to thicken. Glaze should be clear and thick enough to coat the back of a spoon. Remove from the heat and brush generously over grapes and kiwi.

Makes one 9- or 10-inch tart

FIGS STUFFED WITH RASPBERRIES

RASPBERRY SAUCE:

2 pints fresh or two 12-ounce packages frozen raspberries

¼ to ⅓ cup sugar

3 tablespoons Grand Marnier

STUFFED FIGS:

8 to 16 large, ripe figs

4 pints fresh raspberries

Press 2 pints raspberries through a fine sieve into a mixing bowl. Add sugar and Grand Marnier and stir until sugar dissolves. Add additional sugar if necessary, and chill until ready to use.

Cut each fig lengthwise into sixths, starting at the top and cutting to within 1 inch of the base. Place on individual serving plates, spread fig segments out like the petals of a flower, and fill each fig with raspberries. Spoon sauce over and around figs and serve.

Makes 8 servings

Ripe Fig Stuffed with Raspberries.

RASPBERRY CHOCOLATE CAKE

CAKE BATTER:

1	cup flour
2/3	cup cocoa powder
1/4	teaspoon salt
7	eggs, lightly beaten
2	egg yolks, lightly beaten
1	cup granulated sugar
1	teaspoon vanilla extract
3	tablespoons sweet butter, melted and cooled

FILLING:

3/4	cup sweet butter, softened
3/4	cup powdered sugar
1	teaspoon vanilla extract
1	egg
1	egg yolk
3	ounces bittersweet chocolate, melted
1 1/2	tablespoons cocoa powder
1/2	teaspoon powdered instant coffee
1	teaspoon dark rum
	Pinch salt
1/4	cup light rum
1/3	cup raspberry jam, melted

CHOCOLATE LEAVES:

4	ounces semisweet chocolate

CHOCOLATE GLAZE:

5	tablespoons sweet butter
1/4	cup light corn syrup
5	ounces bittersweet chocolate, finely chopped
1	tablespoon light rum
1	pint fresh raspberries

Preheat oven to 350 degrees.

In a large mixing bowl, sift together the flour, cocoa, and salt.

In the top of a double boiler, combine the eggs, egg yolks, sugar, and vanilla and stir over barely simmering water until sugar has dissolved and the mixture is barely warm. Pour into a large mixing bowl and mix with an electric beater at medium speed or with a wire whisk until mixture is very thick and has quadrupled in volume.

Gently fold flour and cocoa mixture, one third at a time, into the batter, until thoroughly incorporated. Quickly fold the melted butter into the batter.

Pour the batter into a thoroughly greased and floured 10-inch round cake pan or springform pan. Place in the oven and bake for about 25 minutes, until the cake springs back when touched lightly in the center. Remove from the oven and let cool for 5 to 10 minutes. Turn cake out onto a wire rack and let cool for at least 2 hours.

Meanwhile, prepare the filling. In a large mixing bowl, cream the butter with an electric beater until light and fluffy. Add the powdered sugar a little at a time, beating thoroughly after each addition. Add the vanilla and beat at high speed for 3 minutes. Add the egg and continue to beat for 2 minutes. Add the egg yolk and beat 2 minutes longer. Add the chocolate, cocoa, and coffee and stir until well blended. Stir in the dark rum and salt.

Using a long, serrated knife, slice the cooled cake horizontally through the center to form two equal layers. Sprinkle the cut side of each layer with the light rum. Spread half of the jam over each layer.

Place one layer, cut side up, on a platter and spread with the butter cream. Place second layer, cut side down, on top of the first. The top of the cake should be flat and even. If it isn't, trim carefully with a serrated knife and brush away crumbs. Refrigerate until thoroughly chilled.

Meanwhile, prepare the chocolate leaves and glaze. For the leaves, melt the 4 ounces of the semisweet chocolate in the top of a double boiler. Brush the melted chocolate quickly over the shiny side of fresh clean leaves (you will need about 12 leaves), being careful not to let the chocolate drip onto the underside of the leaves. Place leaves, chocolate side up, on a baking sheet and chill or freeze until the chocolate has hardened, about 30 minutes or longer.

In a small saucepan, combine the butter and corn syrup for the chocolate glaze and simmer over low heat, stirring constantly for 1 minute.

Remove from the heat and stir in the chocolate and rum. Whisk vigorously until the chocolate is melted and the mixture is very smooth and shiny. Let glaze cool for 8 minutes, then spread it evenly over the top and sides of the cake.

Remove the chocolate leaves from the freezer. Starting at the stem end and working quickly, peel the leaves away from the chocolate.

Arrange the raspberries and chocolate leaves on top of the cake and chill cake for at least 1 hour before serving.

Makes 12-16 servings

Note: This is Wayne Roger's adaptation of Judith Olney's recipe.

FROZEN MOCHA MOUSSE TART WITH CHOCOLATE CURLS

1   recipe pâte brisée (see appendix)

MOCHA MOUSSE FILLING:
6   ounces extra-bittersweet chocolate, such as that made by Lindt
4   tablespoons sweet butter
2   eggs, separated
2   teaspoons instant espresso powder
3   tablespoons hot coffee or espresso
1   tablespoon sugar
½   cup heavy cream, whipped

CHOCOLATE CURLS:
8   ounces semisweet chocolate

A rich tart of Frozen Mocha Mousse capped with chocolate curls.

On a lightly floured surface, roll out pastry to a ⅛-inch thick, 9-by-12-inch rectangle. Fit pastry into an 8-by-11-inch rectangular tart pan with removable bottom. Chill for 10 or 15 minutes.

Preheat oven to 375 degrees. Line pastry shell with aluminum foil and fill with pie weights or dried beans to prevent pastry from puffing up and shrinking while baking. Bake in the center of oven for 15 to 20 minutes. Remove weights and foil and continue to bake shell until crust is golden brown and dry. Let cool before filling.

In a medium saucepan or double boiler over simmering water, heat bittersweet chocolate and butter until melted. Beat egg yolks in a mixing bowl. Gradually whisk chocolate mixture into egg yolks. Dissolve instant espresso in hot coffee and stir into chocolate.

Beat egg whites in a mixing bowl until soft peaks start to form. Add sugar and continue to beat until stiff. Whisk about one third of egg whites into chocolate mixture. Fold in remaining egg whites. Fold whipped cream into mousse. Spoon into cooled tart shell and freeze until firm, at least several hours or overnight.

To make chocolate curls, melt semisweet chocolate in a saucepan or double boiler over simmering water and stir until smooth. Using a rubber spatula, spread melted chocolate ⅟₁₆-inch thick on a smooth-surfaced baking sheet. Chill until chocolate hardens. Remove from refrigerator and let chocolate begin to soften. Using a metal pastry scraper held at a 45 degree angle to the baking sheet, gently loosen and scrape chocolate, with one continuous motion down the length of the baking sheet. If chocolate has reached the proper temperature, it will form small, tight curls. If it cracks, it's too cold; let it warm more. If it sticks to the spatula, it's too warm; chill slightly before continuing. Chill curls until firm.

Remove tart from freezer an hour or so before serving. Decorate with chilled chocolate curls just before serving.

Makes 8 servings

Fruit Cornucopia is an attractive centerpiece for a dessert table.

FRUIT CORNUCOPIA

PASTRY:
- **3** cups flour
- **½** tablespoon sugar
- **¼** teaspoon salt
- **1½** cups cold sweet butter, cut into pieces

GLAZE:
- **2** eggs
- **2** tablespoons heavy cream

In a medium mixing bowl, combine flour, sugar, and salt. Cut in butter with a fork or pastry cutter until mixture resembles coarse meal. Add just enough cold water to moisten dough and make it stick together (3 to 5 tablespoons). Divide in half and form into 2 flat balls. Chill for 30 minutes.

On a lightly floured surface, roll each dough ball out into a ¼-inch thick rectangle 12 by 14 inches. On a baking sheet, stack pastry sheets one on top of the other, each separated by a sheet of waxed paper. Cover top with waxed paper and chill for 15 minutes.

To form cornucopia mold, cut a 12-by-22-inch piece of heavy-duty aluminum foil. Roll into a cone shape 12 inches long by about 6 inches in diameter at the open end. Cut 4 or 5 pieces of foil, 12 by 24 inches, crumple, and stuff them into the cone to help it hold its shape.

Using a sharp knife or pastry cutter, cut each pastry sheet into 14-inch long strips, ⅜ to ½ inch wide. Each rectangle should yield about 24 strips. Place 22 of the pastry strips side by side on a piece of waxed paper on a flat work surface.

Carefully weave remaining pastry strips across first strips, working them over and under bottom layer to form a tight lattice work with as little space as possible between strips. Cover with waxed paper and chill for 15 minutes.

Lay the chilled pastry lattice on a flat surface and remove top sheet of waxed paper. Lay foil cornucopia mold diagonally across lattice with its open end pointing toward the bottom left-hand corner of lattice. Gently fold the top left corner of lattice over the cornucopia mold, toward bottom right corner. Continue to roll cornucopia toward bottom right corner, tucking in ends of pastry as you roll. With moistened fingers, firmly tuck in any loose pastry ends at tip or seam of cone. At open edge, fold loose ends back on top of themselves and crimp to make secure. Braid remaining 2 strips and use as a decorative edge, moistening it with cold water to affix. Place seam-side down on a large baking sheet and chill for 30 minutes.

Preheat oven to 375 degrees.

In a small bowl, beat the eggs and cream together until well blended and brush generously over cornucopia. Bake for 20 to 25 minutes, or until golden brown. Let cool completely.

Carefully pull out foil stuffing from center of mold. Loosen mold from sides of pastry, being very careful not to break pastry. Gently collapse and remove foil. Fill cornucopia with seasonal fruits and berries and serve with generous amounts of softly whipped cream. Pieces of the cornucopia are served with each portion of fruit.

Makes 10 to 12 servings

CASSIS SORBET

1   33-ounce jar black currants in heavy syrup
3   tablespoons sugar
3   tablespoons crème de cassis

Drain currants and pour syrup into a saucepan. Add sugar, bring mixture to a boil and boil over high heat until reduced by one third.

Meanwhile, place currants in a food processor and purée until smooth. Press purée through a medium sieve, then through a fine sieve, discarding seeds and skins.

Combine syrup, currant purée, and crème de cassis in a mixing bowl and chill thoroughly.

Place chilled mixture in an ice cream machine and prepare according to manufacturer's directions.

Makes 1½ quarts

GOOSEBERRY BARQUETTES

1   recipe pâte brisée (see appendix)

PASTRY CREAM:
⅓   cup sugar
1   tablespoon plus 2 teaspoons cornstarch
     Pinch salt
1   cup plus 2 tablespoons milk
2   egg yolks, beaten
1   tablespoon butter, softened
1   teaspoon rum
½   cup heavy cream, whipped

TO ASSEMBLE:
1   pint fresh gooseberries, peeled and sliced
1   10-ounce jar clear apple jelly
1   bunch fresh mint leaves

On a lightly floured surface, roll out pâte brisée dough to a ⅛-inch thick rectangle. Place 12 3-inch barquette pans side by side, in 2 rows of 6 on a clean surface. Lay pastry over the top of barquettes and run rolling pin across the top to cut pastry to fit pans. Gently press pastry into barquettes with your fingers. Chill for 30 minutes.

In a small mixing bowl, combine sugar, cornstarch, and salt. Add 2 tablespoons of the milk and blend well. Set aside. In a medium saucepan, heat remaining milk over medium heat until almost boiling. Stir in cornstarch mixture and simmer, whisking constantly, until mixture begins to thicken. Remove from the heat and stir in egg yolks, butter, and rum. Let cool.

Preheat oven to 375 degrees.

Line each chilled barquette with a sheet of aluminum foil and fill with pie weights or dried beans to prevent pastry from puffing up and shrinking during baking. Place on a baking sheet in the middle of the oven and bake for 12 to 15 minutes, or until lightly browned. Let cool.

Fold whipped cream into the pastry cream and spoon into a pastry bag fitted with a plain tip. Pipe cream into cooled barquette shells.

Arrange gooseberry slices in barquettes, standing them as close together as possible, at a 45 degree angle.

In a small saucepan, melt the jelly over medium-low heat. Stir 2 teaspoons in water and simmer until mixture thickens and coats the back of a spoon. Spoon or brush glaze generously over gooseberries. Garnish with mint sprigs.

Makes 12 individual barquettes

Note: These are best if served within one or two hours of making.

MILLE ET UNE FEUILLES

1 recipe puff pastry (see appendix)

PASTRY CREAM:
1 cup milk
1 vanilla bean
¼ cup plus 1 tablespoon sugar
3 egg yolks
1 tablespoon rice flour
1 tablespoon cornstarch
1 teaspoon sweet butter
1 cup heavy cream, softy whipped

TO SERVE:
Powdered sugar for sprinkling
1 pint golden raspberries

On a lightly floured surface, roll pastry into a ¾-inch thick rectangle and cut in thirds. Roll out each third (refrigerating remaining two thirds in the meantime so they don't become too warm) to a ⅟₁₆-inch thick rectangle about 5 by 18 inches. For easy handling, cut rectangles in half, forming six 5-by-9-inch pieces. Place these pieces, spacing them evenly, on baking sheets. Chill for at least 30 minutes.

Meanwhile, prepare pastry cream. In a small saucepan, combine milk, vanilla bean, and ¼ cup of the sugar and bring to a boil. In a small bowl, beat egg yolks with the remaining tablespoon sugar until thick. Sprinkle rice flour and cornstarch over egg yolks and beat until well blended. Remove vanilla bean from milk and beat a small amount of hot milk into egg yolk mixture. Pour egg mixture into saucepan with remaining hot milk and bring to a boil, stirring vigorously to prevent scorching. Pour into a mixing bowl; rub top of mixture with butter to prevent a skin from forming. Cover with plastic wrap and let cool completely.

Preheat oven to 425 degrees.

Prick chilled pastry with a fork and bake in the center of the oven for about 20 minutes, or until evenly browned. Transfer to wire racks and let cool.

When ready to assemble, fold whipped cream into the cold pastry cream. Spread a ½-inch layer of pastry cream over all but 2 of the pastry strips and stack them one on top of the other in 2 stacks, topping each stack with one of the 2 plain pastry strips. Sprinkle powdered sugar over the top of each stack and decorate with raspberries. Using a serrated knife, cut each stack into 4 pieces, each about 5 by 2 inches.

Makes 8 servings

ORANGE CURD TART

½ recipe pâte brisée sucrée (see appendix)
¼ recipe puff pastry (see appendix)

ORANGE CURD:
1 cup sugar
6 egg yolks, lightly beaten and strained
½ cup freshly squeezed orange juice
2 tablespoons grated orange zest
2 tablespoons Grand Marnier
½ cup sweet butter, cut into pieces and softened

EGG WASH:
1 egg, lightly beaten
2 tablespoons heavy cream

TO ASSEMBLE:
6 navel oranges
4 tablespoons Grand Marnier
1 cup orange marmalade

On a lightly floured surface, roll pâte brisée out to a ⅛-inch thick rectangle about 9-by-13 inches. Using a sharp knife, trim rectangle evenly to 8-by-13 inches. Roll puff pastry out to a ⅛-inch thick strip about 12 inches long. Cut into 4 1-inch wide strips and lay on the four sides of pâte brisée rectangle to form edges, moistening the edges of the two pastries with cold water to make them stick together. Trim to fit. Prick bottom of tart shell with a fork and chill for 30 minutes.

Meanwhile, prepare orange curd. Combine sugar and egg yolks in a small saucepan and whisk lightly. Whisk in orange juice and zest, and Grand Marnier. Place over a very low heat or over a pan of simmering water and warm, whisking constantly until mixture thickens and coats the back of a spoon; do not allow to boil. Remove from heat and add butter, a few pieces at a time, whisking vigorously after each addition until butter is completely incorporated into egg yolks. Let cool. Chill until ready to fill tart.

Working over a bowl, peel oranges, removing all of the white pith. Separate oranges into segments, removing membrane with a sharp paring knife, and place segments in the bowl. Sprinkle with 3 tablespoons of the Grand Marnier,

cover and chill for at least 2 hours before finishing tart.

Preheat oven to 400 degrees. Blend the egg and cream together and brush over the edges of the pastry. Bake pastry shell for 15 to 20 minutes or until golden brown. Let cool.

Drain marinated orange segments and pat dry on paper towel. Spread orange curd over the bottom of the tart shell. Arrange orange segments as closely together as possible in a decorative pattern on top of orange curd. Melt marmalade and remaining tablespoon of Grand Marnier in a small saucepan and spoon or brush generously over top of the oranges. Chill for 30 minutes before serving.

Makes 6 servings

PITHIVIERS
(Almond Puff)

4 tablespoons sweet butter, softened
¼ cup sugar
1 egg
½ cup finely ground blanched almonds
¼ teaspoon almond extract
1 tablespoon dark rum
1½ recipes puff pastry (see appendix)

GLAZE:
1 egg yolk
2 tablespoons heavy cream

In a small mixing bowl, cream butter and sugar together until light and fluffy. Add egg and beat until smooth. Stir in almonds, almond extract, and rum. Form into a ball, wrap in plastic wrap and chill until firm.

On a lightly floured work surface, roll pastry out to a ⅛-inch thick, 15-inch square. Place chilled almond paste in the center of dough. Gather up corners of pastry and tie at center securely with heavy cotton string, making sure that almond paste is totally enclosed by pastry. Cut off excess pastry with pinking shears and place puff on a parchment-covered baking sheet. Chill for at least 2 hours.

Preheat oven to 450 degrees.

Blend egg yolk with cream and brush over pastry. Bake in the center of the oven for 20 minutes at 450 degrees, then reduce heat to 425 degrees and continue baking until pastry is a golden brown.

Remove from the oven and slide puff onto a rack to cool. Serve slightly warm or at room temperature. Garnish, if desired, with a single fresh flower blossom.

Makes 8 to 10 servings

A golden Pithiviers purse with a buttery, almond filling.

POACHED PEARS

2   cups red wine
2   tablespoons fresh lemon juice
1   cup sugar
1   cinnamon stick
    Finely grated zest of 1 lemon
1   vanilla bean
8   Bosc pears, peeled, stems left on (see note)

In a large heavy saucepan or Dutch oven, combine wine, lemon juice, sugar, cinnamon stick, lemon zest, and vanilla bean and bring to a boil over high heat. Reduce heat, place pears, stem-end up, in wine mixture, and add enough water to cover them completely. Simmer slowly over low heat for 10 to 20 minutes, or until pears are just tender.

Remove pears and place in a shallow serving dish. Increase heat under saucepan, bring poaching liquid to a boil and continue to boil until reduced to about 1 cup. Pour reduced liquid over pears. Serve warm or cold.

Makes 8 servings

Note: Be careful to peel pears as uniformly as possible for an attractive presentation.

SHELL-SHAPED DACQUOISE

MERINGUES:

6 egg whites
¼ teaspoon cream of tartar
Pinch salt
1 teaspoon almond extract
1½ cups sugar
⅔ cup cornstarch
½ cup finely ground roasted hazelnuts or almonds

COFFEE BUTTER CREAM FILLING:

5 eggs
¾ cup sugar
2 cups sweet butter, slightly softened, and cut into pieces
1 tablespoon instant espresso coffee
2 tablespoons Cognac

TO ASSEMBLE:

8 ounces semisweet chocolate, melted
Powdered sugar

Sketch a scallop shell about 7 inches across on parchment and cut out. Line 2 large baking sheets with parchment. Trace 1 scallop shell onto the center of parchment on 1 baking sheet. On the second baking sheet, trace 2 scallop shells, leaving space between them.

Preheat oven to 300 degrees.

In a medium mixing bowl, combine egg whites, cream of tartar, salt, and almond extract and beat until soft peaks form. Add 1 cup of the sugar, 1 tablespoon at a time, continuing to beat with an electric mixer at high speed until dry and very stiff.

Combine remaining ½ cup sugar, cornstarch, and ground nuts in a small bowl and fold into meringue.

Spoon mixture into a pastry bag fitted with a plain round tip ½ inch in diameter (#7). Pipe long fingers, slightly less than ½ inch thick, from the scalloped edge of shell pattern to the base of shell. Fill in where necessary with meringue. Starting ½ inch from scalloped edge, pipe another layer of meringue directly on top of the first layer, filling in where necessary. Starting ½ inch from outside edge of second layer, pipe on a third layer. Pipe one layer of meringue on each of 2 remaining scallop shell patterns. Pipe any remaining meringue in strands on the baking sheet for decoration.

Place the meringues in center of oven and bake until stiff and dry, at least 3 hours. Turn off oven and let meringues sit overnight, or until completely cool. Remove meringues from parchment.

To make butter cream, beat eggs and sugar together in a small saucepan and warm over low heat until sugar dissolves. Remove from the heat and beat with an electric mixer at high speed until cooled. Add butter, piece by piece, and continue to beat at low speed until butter cream is light and fluffy. Dissolve espresso in Cognac and beat into butter cream.

To assemble dacquoise, spread the two single layers of meringue with a thin coat of melted chocolate, followed by a generous layer of butter cream. Place one on top of the other and top with the triple layer meringue shell. Spread remaining butter cream over sides of shell. Crumble extra meringue strands between your fingers or with a rolling pin and press into the butter-cream-covered sides. Sift powdered sugar over top of the meringue shell. Chill until ready to serve. To keep longer than six hours, wrap very well with plastic wrap and freeze for up to 4 days. Bring to cool room temperature and cut with sharp serrated knife.

Makes 8 to 10 servings

STRAWBERRY TART IN AN ALMOND NUT CRUST

CRUST:

1	cup finely ground blanched almonds
½	cup sweet butter, softened
4	tablespoons sugar
1½	cups flour
1	egg, beaten
½	teaspoon vanilla extract

FILLING:

3	pints fresh, ripe strawberries
1	6-ounce jar red currant jelly
1	tablespoon unflavored gelatin
¼	cup Grand Marnier

In a medium mixing bowl, combine almonds, butter, sugar, flour, egg, and vanilla extract and blend together well. Press mixture into a 9-inch tart pan with a removable bottom, being careful to keep thickness of the crust uniform. Chill for 30 minutes.

Preheat oven to 350 degrees.

Bake in the center of the oven for 15 to 20 minutes, or until crust is light golden brown. Let cool before filling.

Hull the strawberries and arrange them stem-end down in the cooled crust, starting at center and continuing in a spiral pattern to edge of crust.

In a small saucepan, combine jelly, gelatin, and Grand Marnier and stir over low heat until mixture is thick and clear. Spoon or brush generously over the tops of the berries.

Remove tart from pan before serving, and garnish, if desired, with nasturtium blossoms.

Makes 6 to 8 servings

RHUBARB SORBET

2 ¾   cups sugar
1   pound fresh rhubarb, washed and cut
        into ½-inch pieces
        Juice of 1 lemon

In a medium saucepan, combine 2 cups of the sugar with 1 cup of water and bring to a boil over high heat, without stirring, but shaking the pan to dissolve the sugar. Remove from the heat when the liquid is clear and syrupy and let cool.

In a separate saucepan, combine the rhubarb and remaining ¾ cup of sugar and cook, stirring occasionally, over low heat until the rhubarb is tender, 15 to 20 minutes. Taste for sweetness, adding more sugar if necessary. Remove from the heat and let cool, preferably overnight.

In a large mixing bowl, combine the sugar syrup, rhubarb, and lemon juice. Pour the mixture into an ice cream freezer and freeze according to manufacturer's instructions.

Makes 10 servings

PHYLLO TARTS

PHYLLO SHELLS:
6   sheets phyllo dough
6   tablespoons sweet butter, clarified, for
     brushing (see appendix)

FILLING:
1½ cups crème fraîche (see appendix)
1   teaspoon honey
2   pints fresh strawberries, hulled and sliced

GLAZE:
½   cup currant jelly

Preheat oven to 350 degrees.

Carefully unfold phyllo dough and spread it out on a flat work surface. Peel off one sheet of phyllo at a time and cover remaining sheets with a damp towel to prevent them from drying and cracking. Cut each sheet into six 6-by-3-inch strips. Brush strips with clarified butter. Place one strip, buttered side up, on work surface in front of you. Lay another strip, buttered side up, across first strip at a quarter turn so that the corners do not overlap. Lay on four more buttered phyllo strips, turning each a quarter turn away from the last to form a 6-inch circle. Carefully invert circle and press into a 4-inch round buttered tart pan with removable bottom. Press phyllo leaves down gently but firmly against fluted sides and bottom of pan. Brush inside of tart shell with melted butter. Prepare 5 more tart pans in this manner with remaining phyllo strips. Using scissors, trim edges of tart shells unevenly to form decorative ragged edges. Line each tart shell with a sheet of waxed paper and fill with pie weights or dried beans. Place tart shells on a large baking sheet and bake in the center of oven for 10 minutes. Remove waxed paper and weights and continue baking until golden brown, about 5 minutes. Let cool.

Meanwhile, whip crème fraîche and honey together until stiff; do not overwhip or crème fraîche will become runny. Divide crème fraîche among the 6 tart shells, spreading it smoothly over the bottom of each. Arrange strawberry slices, as close together as possible, in tart shells in a spiral or other decorative pattern.

In a small saucepan, melt jelly with 2 tablespoons water over medium heat, stirring constantly until it begins to boil and thickens enough to coat the back of a spoon. Brush glaze generously over strawberries.

Makes 6 individual tarts

TALE OF A TUG

TUGBOAT DINNER

Oysters on the Half Shell with
Black Caviar

Radicchio with Creamed Morels

Quails with Foie Gras

Haricots Verts and Mushroom Salad

Seafood Ragout

Fresh Raspberry Tart

While bare feet in the wet sand and a blueberry pie aptly epitomize some of the best summer pleasures, there are occasional moments in this season of improvisation when our spirits crave a more formal mode of expression. If the first is as the sound of a Scott Joplin rag, spontaneous and carefree in feeling, the second is Cole Porter, suave and consistently elegant. Warm weather offers a multitude of options for elegant outdoor entertaining, whether in a sunny garden plot, on a white sandy beach, or a patio by a lake. Balmy twilights only enhance the refinement of tables set with delicate china and crystal, impeccably selected foods and wines, and the entire panoply of adornments that characterize elegant occasions.

The East River of Manhattan provided a luminous setting for one version of outdoor formality, held on an evening in June. Invitations for the event, sent a few weeks in advance, simply directed the eight guests to meet at a specified pier by the river at 6:30 P.M., formal attire requested. As the group assembles, the lengthening rays of the late afternoon sun cast dramatic shadows. A red and black tugboat waits at the dock for the party to embark on an elegant, floating dinner party, with the passing sights of New York Harbor as background and later on, a full moon for illumination.

As guests climb aboard, they are escorted to the stern where a single round table has been carefully set. Gold-rimmed, cobalt blue dinner plates and delicate stemware have been placed on an Art Deco-inspired cotton tablecloth. The hostess, Hilary Cushing, Director of Special Events at Sotheby Parke Bernet, has contributed her collection of bone-handled knives and collaborated on the centerpiece, a giant clam shell filled with fresh grapes and white orchids.

Tonight's food and service are being provided by Glorious Food, a New York catering firm. Executive chef and co-owner Jean-Claude Nédélec began with extensive advance preparation in his professional kitchen and will finish the last-minute details in the tug's tiny galley. To minimize the shipboard work, Hilary and Chef Nédélec decided on a selection of hot and cold items, many of which could be assembled ahead. Scallops, mussels, and fresh fish from local waters; ripe red raspberries; and earthy wild mushrooms, all in abundant supply now, are the ingredients for this multi-course repast.

Oysters on the half-shell, dolloped with black caviar to enhance their briny flavor, are served on a bed of ice as a simple first course requiring little more than a pair of experienced hands in the galley to shuck the fresh mollusks. The oysters are accompanied by glasses of chilled Dom Ruinart (1975). Next appear crisp and colorful radicchio leaves filled with a quick sauté of nutty-flavored morels and shallots, napped with heavy cream

The din of rush hour in Manhattan seems already leagues away as guests embark on the tug.

and chives.

As the tugboat begins its harbor cruise, gliding slowly under New York's landmark bridges—Williamsburg, Manhattan, and Brooklyn—the next course is served by a trio of white-gloved waiters. Inspired by the fresh foie gras that has only recently been produced in this country, Nédélec has stuffed tender young quail with a mixture of the suc-culent fattened duck liver and black truffles and roasted them in advance. At serving time, the moist pink meat is sliced and small portions are presented on a bed of golden aspic cubes, along with a tart Cumberland Sauce. It is accompanied by a salad of fresh haricots verts and a robust Châteauneuf du Pape (1975). Diners enjoy these elegant offerings as waves gently lap the sides of the tug, and

Under the supervision of Chef Jean-Claude Nédélec dinner provisions are loaded on board.

Opposite: Pearl-handled flatware, golden-rimmed dinner plates, and a sea shell centerpiece with grapes and orchids set an opulent stage for dinner.

overhead, a solitary seagull laments the party's invasion of its domain.

The main course has been prepared on board and is presented steaming hot in its handsome copper cooking skillet. The Seafood Ragout includes bite-size morsels of seabass and red snapper, mussels, and an assortment of other shellfish poached in a wonderfully fragrant broth seasoned with saffron, Pernod, tomatoes, and garlic. To accompany this savory stew are loaves of hot, crusty French bread and the traditional Provençal condiment for fish ragout, *rouille*, a pungent mixture of garlic, olive oil, egg, and red pepper, made in advance and chilled, then brought to room temperature before serving. A white wine from Burgundy, Meursault Terrières (1982), is served with the ragout.

After the dinner, guests stroll to the upper deck where chilled Champagne and a light puff pastry tart with fresh raspberries and brandy-scented crème fraîche have been set out. The tug approaches the Statue of Liberty, which seems passively to bestow her approval on the festivities. Elegant evening gowns rustle, stirred by the temperate night winds, as female guests and their tuxedoed escorts take an after-dinner promenade. Soon the tug turns slowly around, to retrace its journey back to the dock.

A first course of oysters dolloped with caviar.

QUAILS WITH FOIE GRAS

10 quails
    Salt
    Freshly ground black pepper
1 pound fresh foie gras, sliced into about 20 pieces
2 black truffles, cut into julienne strips (optional)
3 tablespoons clarified butter
½ cup diced carrots
½ cup diced celery
½ cup diced onions

TO SERVE:
    Cumberland sauce (recipe follows)

Preheat oven to 400 degrees.

Using a small, sharp boning knife, make an incision down the back of each quail and cut down both sides of backbone. Cut meat away from the rib cage, working as close to the bone as possible and being careful not to puncture flesh and skin of bird. Lift out the carcass.

Lay each bird, skin side down, on a flat surface. Season lightly with salt and pepper. Place a slice of foie gras in the center of each quail. Sprinkle with truffle pieces, add a second foie gras slice, and finish with a layer of truffle pieces. Fold the quail over the stuffing and truss securely down the back.

Place the birds in a roasting pan and brush with 2 tablespoons of clarified butter. Place in oven and bake for 10 minutes.

Meanwhile, heat remaining tablespoon of butter in a large, heavy skillet. Add carrots, celery, and onions and sauté over medium heat until golden brown. Remove roasting pan from oven and reduce heat to 350 degrees. Lift quails out of pan. Spread sautéed vegetables over bottom of pan, lay birds on top of vegetables, and return pan to the oven for 10 minutes.

Let quails cool slightly, then refrigerate, covered, overnight. (Discard the sautéed vegetables or reserve them for another use.) Remove trussing and arrange birds (whole or sliced) on a serving platter. Serve cold with Cumberland sauce.

Makes 10 servings

Cumberland Sauce

½ cup red currant jelly
    Juice of 2 oranges
    Juice of 1 lemon
1 tablespoon finely chopped shallots
    Zest of 1 orange, cut into julienne strips
    Zest of ½ lemon, cut into julienne strips
2 teaspoons dry mustard
¼ teaspoon ground ginger
    Pinch cayenne pepper
¼ cup port

In a medium saucepan, combine the jelly, orange and lemon juices, and shallots and simmer over a low heat until reduced by half. In a separate saucepan, blanch orange and lemon zest in rapidly boiling water for about 2 minutes. Drain and set aside.

Combine the mustard, ginger, cayenne, and port in a small mixing bowl and blend well. Add to the reduced sauce and bring to a boil, stirring constantly. Remove from heat immediately and cool. Stir in the blanched citrus zest.

Serve at room temperature with game or poultry.

Makes about 1 cup

RADICCHIO WITH CREAMED MORELS

½   cup dried morels (see note)
1   to 2 heads radicchio (about 20 leaves)
1   tablespoon butter
1   tablespoon shallots, finely chopped
1   cup heavy cream
     Salt
     Freshly ground black pepper
     Chopped chives, for garnish

Place morels in a small glass bowl and add enough boiling water to cover. Let stand covered for 30 to 45 minutes, until reconstituted. Drain and gently squeeze out excess water.

Carefully separate radicchio leaves, rinse with cold water, and dry thoroughly. Melt butter in a large, heavy skillet; add shallots and sauté over low heat until softened. Add morels and cream, season with salt and pepper, and simmer over low to medium heat until sauce thickens, about 10 minutes.

Arrange radicchio leaves on a serving platter or individual serving plates and spoon a small amount of the mushroom mixture into each. Sprinkle with chives and serve warm.

Makes 10 servings

Note: 2 cups of fresh morels, chanterelles, or other wild mushrooms may be substituted for dried.

Crisp radicchio leaves enclose sautéed morels with cream.

The main course is Seafood Ragout, enhanced with saffron and served with Rouille and toasted bread slices.

SEAFOOD RAGOUT

1   cup olive oil
1   cup sliced onions
1   cup sliced carrots
1   cup sliced celery
1   cup julienned leeks
8   cups court bouillon (recipe follows)
1   clove garlic, minced
    Pinch saffron
1   tablespoon Pernod (optional)
1½ pounds filleted and skinned red snapper,
      cut into 2-by-3-inch pieces
1½ pounds filleted and skinned sea bass, cut
      into 2-by-3-inch pieces
1   pound sea scallops, washed
1   pound medium shrimp, peeled and
      deveined

1   dozen mussels in the shell, scrubbed and
      debearded
1   dozen littleneck clams in the shell, scrubbed
2   small tomatoes, cut into wedges
1   tablespoon finely chopped parsley

TO SERVE:
    Small boiled potatoes
    Toasted French bread
    Rouille (recipe follows)

Heat the oil in a large stainless steel or enameled kettle. Add the onions, carrots, celery, and leeks and sauté, stirring, over a low heat until softened, about 5 minutes. Add 4 cups of the court bouillon and simmer for 20 minutes. Stir in the garlic, saffron, and Pernod; reduce heat to very low and keep warm while poaching fish and shellfish.

Heat 3 cups of the court bouillon in a large skillet and individually poach snapper, bass, scallops, and shrimp until just cooked, about 2 to 3 minutes each. Remove with a slotted spoon to a platter and keep warm. Heat the remaining cup of court bouillon in a large saucepan. Add mussels and clams; cover and simmer over medium heat until shells open, about 5 minutes. (Discard any mussels or clams that do not open.) Remove with a slotted spoon to a platter and keep warm. Strain the poaching liquid from fish and shellfish through a fine sieve lined with cheesecloth. Add strained liquid to the soup base and simmer over medium heat until warmed through.

Arrange fish, shellfish, and tomato wedges on a large, deep serving platter or in a soup terrine and ladle soup base over them. Sprinkle with parsley. Serve with small, peeled boiled potatoes and thinly sliced, toasted French bread spread with rouille.

Makes 10 servings

Court Bouillon

6 cups dry white wine
6 cups water
1 cup chopped leek greens
1 cup chopped carrots
1 cup chopped celery
1 cup chopped fennel leaves
3 cloves garlic, crushed
½ cup chopped parsley stems (optional)
3 bay leaves
1 teaspoon cracked black peppercorns

½ teaspoon dried thyme
Salt to taste

Place all ingredients in a large enameled or stainless steel kettle or Dutch oven and bring to a boil over medium heat. Reduce heat and let simmer, partially covered, for about 20 minutes. Strain through a fine-mesh sieve lined with several layers of cheesecloth. (Do not force liquid through sieve; let it drain slowly or liquid will be cloudy.) Discard solids and use court bouillon as directed in individual recipes.

Makes about 2 quarts (8 cups)

Rouille

1 red pepper, roasted, peeled, and seeded
1 jalapeño chili, roasted, peeled, and seeded
4 cloves garlic, finely chopped
2 egg yolks
1 tablespoon fresh French bread crumbs
Pinch salt
1 cup olive oil

Combine peppers, garlic, egg yolks, bread crumbs, and salt in a food processor fitted with a metal blade, or an electric blender, and process until smooth. With motor running, add olive oil in a slow, steady stream and process until thoroughly incorporated.

Rouille will keep, covered and refrigerated, for about 5 days. Bring to room temperature before stirring and serving. Serve with Seafood Ragout or other fish soups and stews.

Makes about 1¼ cups

HARICOTS VERTS AND MUSHROOM SALAD

1   pound haricots verts or young green beans, trimmed and washed
½   teaspoon finely chopped shallots
¼   teaspoon salt
     Pinch freshly ground black pepper
2   tablespoons olive oil
1   tablespoon tarragon vinegar
¼   pound mushrooms, wiped clean and cut into julienne strips
1   black truffle, cut into julienne strips (optional)

Cook beans in a large saucepan of boiling salted water until crisp-tender, about 2 to 4 minutes. Rinse in cold water, drain, and let cool.

Combine the shallots, salt, pepper, olive oil, and vinegar in a large mixing bowl. Add beans and toss. Gently fold in the mushrooms and truffle and serve at room temperature.

Makes 10 servings

FRESH RASPBERRY TART

1   pound puff pastry dough (see appendix)

FILLING:
2   cups crème fraîche (see appendix)
2   tablespoons superfine sugar
3   tablespoons Framboise or raspberry brandy
2   pints fresh raspberries, cleaned and hulled (but not washed)

GLAZE:
¼   cup red currant jelly

Preheat oven to 400 degrees.

On a lightly floured work surface, roll out puff pastry dough into a round approximately 16 inches in diameter and ⅛ inch thick. Transfer to a large baking sheet, cover with plastic wrap, and chill in freezer until firm, about 10 minutes. Trim edge evenly and brush a 1-inch border all around with ice water. Fold border over to form a stand-up edge and press gently to

seal. Trim 1/16 inch off border (cutting off fold allows pastry to rise evenly) and score border with a design if desired. Prick bottom of tart with a fork to prevent bubbling. Cover with plastic wrap and chill in the freezer 10 minutes longer.

Bake on the bottom rack of the oven for 10 minutes. Reduce heat to 350 degrees and bake 15 minutes longer, or until golden brown. Remove from oven and cool.

In a medium mixing bowl, combine the crème fraîche, sugar, and 2 tablespoons of Framboise.

Just before serving, spoon the crème fraîche mixture into pastry shell and spread evenly over bottom with the back of a spoon. Starting at the center of tart and working toward edge, arrange raspberries as close together as possible in a spiral pattern until all the crème is covered.

In a small saucepan, heat currant jelly and remaining tablespoon of Framboise just until jelly is melted. Brush glaze gently over tops of raspberries and serve.

Makes one 15-inch tart

What better way to enjoy New York in June?

A U T U M N   B A C C H A N A L

VINEYARD PICNIC

Butter Lettuce Stuffed with Corn Salad

Whole Wheat French Bread with
Raisins and Walnuts

Dorian Leigh Parker's Torta Rustica

Roasted Squabs with Concord Grape
and Leek Sauce

Vegetable Tian

Concord Grape Pie

As if to divert our thoughts from the harsh imminence of winter, autumn presents itself as the most winsome of seasons. Farms and orchards that range in size from garden plots to small towns yield an abundance of crops ready to be gathered: Rome Beauties as big as baseballs and claret-colored Winesap apples, Anjou and Bosc pears are ripe for picking in New England orchards, while on midwestern farms, acres of newly picked corn fill the air with a fresh warm scent. Greenmarkets and local farmstands entice passers-by with their fresh produce.

Abundance stimulates a mood of sharing, and there is something easy and natural about entertaining at this time of year. The climate is a near perfect blend of warm sunlight and fresh breezes that makes the outdoors an excellent setting for feasting and relaxing. There is a spirit of reunion in the air. Friends have returned from vacations, and schools and colleges haven't yet gotten underway; everyone is back home for a while and in good spirits for an old-fashioned family picnic.

There are a few guidelines to follow when entertaining outdoors in the fall. Cooler weather sparks robust appetites, so autumn menus should offer plenty of substantial food, including one or two hearty entrées and hot items, for example a soup or a bracing beverage such as mulled wine, both of which can be transported and kept warm in thermoses. Those chutneys and wonderfully aromatic fruit conserves that have just been put up for winter make excellent accompaniments for picnic feasts, so tuck a few jars into picnic hampers for friends to sample and enjoy. To complement these fuller menus, more extensive table settings with interesting serving platters, utensils, and floral accents are suitable even for portable feasts. Pretty linens and antiques add richness and warmth that is in keeping with the more deliberate, formal mood of this season.

To Susan and Hugh Connell, owners of the seven-year-old Crosswoods Winery in North Stonington, Connecticut, autumn entertaining is a grand tradition. Come September each year, just as the grapes start to sag in heavy clusters waiting to be picked, the Connells fete the harvest, inviting guests to share with them a toast to the new wine that October will bring.

It is a lazy Sunday afternoon, and within the roomy kitchen of the Connells' late-Victorian farmhouse, friends arrive with last-minute contributions—compotes of grape jam, juicy white peaches, sheaves of fresh rosemary and lavender. The children of the group form a bucket brigade of hands to shift the food and drink from indoors, outside and onto the back of an oak flatbed harnessed to an old Chevy pickup. When everything is assembled, the truck eases slowly onto the roadway, passing pigs on the left, a cornfield on the right, and turns carefully into a small clearing in the vineyard.

A flatbed truck carts lunch provisions to the vineyard.

In contrast to the highly developed California wine industry, viticulture in the Northeast is still a pioneer business. Crosswoods is one of twenty-two wineries in New England, and, like many other fledgling winemakers, the Connells frequently play host to visitors who come to share the excitement of this new enterprise built on the site of a turn-of-the-century dairy farm. They also come to enjoy the pleasures of the Connells' table. Food is serious business at Crosswoods, where menus are planned to complement the new wines as well as to take advantage of seasonal vegetables from the abundant gardens, pork from the piggery, and eggs and chickens from the coops.

Today, after a preprandial amble through the vineyards to admire the grapes—Gamay,

Fragrant Belle of Georgia peaches from a neighbor's orchard.

Beaujolais, Pinot Noir, Johannisberg Riesling, Gewürztraminer, and a new varietal, Scrimshaw White—guests are hungry and ready for a picnic in the Connells' style, extravagant and plentiful; the kind of lunch where a hungry ten-year-old can, if he feels like it, steal a piece of pie before dinner and no one will mind, and where there is enough food to last through hours of lazing in the afternoon sun.

The Connells' flatbed, now adorned with an early American coverlet, has been pressed into use as a portable buffet, and its cargo is a feast of international and regional dishes complemented by a selection of Crosswood's wines. This is a party to pay homage to the grapes, and the celebratory spirit is reflected in both food and table setting. The aroma of a trailing centerpiece of fresh herbs—sage, mint, and thyme—displayed in an American antique kitchen bowl whets guests' appetites.

Blue and white checked cotton napkins, silver utensils in small baskets, and a tall stack of heirloom Quimper dinner plates are all quickly put to use as guests help themselves to the appetizers. These include sandwiches of flaky caraway scones filled with smoked turkey and tart gamay grape jam arranged in a copper tray, and bronze-hued tea eggs piled high in an antique yellowware pottery bowl. A fruity Gewürztraminer accompanies the sandwiches and eggs. Extra-large vine baskets make handsome containers for braids of Whole Wheat Bread with Raisins and Walnuts, spread with creamy white farm butter. The nutty bread is delicious with a salad of sweet, picked-that-morning white corn scraped from the cob, mixed with slivers of red pepper, and scooped into cups of tender butter lettuce. An adaptation of a French favorite, Vegetable Tian, includes homegrown broccoli and zucchini topped with a light egg custard, and served at room temperature. Another European-inspired offering, Italian Torta Rustica, has a butter-rich domed pastry shell filled with colorful layers of omelet, mozzarella, spinach, and fresh salmon.

Grape leaves are used to decorate the buffet, to garnish the food, and also to envelop the plump, locally grown squab that have been rubbed with garlic and thyme, roasted in advance, and wrapped in the leaves to help them retain their juices and stay slightly warm. Their delicate flavor is enhanced by a mahogany-colored sauce, made of the pan

This specimen from Hugh Connell's vintage auto collection finds an appreciative audience.

drippings, Armagnac, and grapes, which is passed separately for serving case. Estate-bottled Gamay Beaujolais Nouveau is an excellent choice for the main course. A New England classic, Concord Grape Pie, purply-black in color with a dense, winy flavor that is intoxicatingly rich is a superb coda to this harvest menu.

Children wander off to play on the hillside, to snatch a warm egg from an irate hen in the coop, or to take a ride in one of Hugh Connell's vintage autos. Hosts and friends relax, meandering through the vineyard, sipping chilled Johannisberg Riesling as they stroll. A guest returns to the buffet for a cold drumstick of squab. The sun sets early this evening and the night air is slightly chilly. Soon it will be October.

Soft butter lettuce stuffed with fresh sweet corn.

BUTTER LETTUCE STUFFED WITH CORN SALAD

8   small (3-inch diameter) heads butter lettuce
8   to 10 medium ears sweet corn, husked
⅓   cup olive oil
3   sprigs fresh rosemary or ½ teaspoon
     dried
2   to 3 cloves garlic, minced
4   to 5 tablespoons red wine vinegar
3   tablespoons chopped fresh basil
    Salt

Freshly ground black pepper
2   red peppers, seeded and finely chopped
     (optional)
4   to 5 scallions, chopped (optional)

Remove any bruised outer leaves from lettuce and rinse thoroughly, keeping heads intact and being careful not to break leaves. Invert heads in a colander or on paper towels and let drain thoroughly.

Drop corn into a large pot of boiling water. Let water return to a boil, cover, turn off heat and let stand for 10 to 15 minutes, until tender. Remove corn and blot dry with paper towel. Cut kernels from the cobs and place in a mixing bowl.

Heat oil in a small skillet. Add rosemary and garlic and gently sauté over low heat for 3 to 4 minutes. Pour over the corn. Add vinegar and chopped basil, season with salt and pepper, and toss well. Add chopped red pepper and chopped scallions, if desired, and toss again.

Gently open lettuce heads and spoon a generous amount of the corn salad into the heart of each. Serve immediately.

Makes 8 servings

WHOLE WHEAT FRENCH BREAD WITH RAISINS AND WALNUTS

3   packages active dry yeast
2   tablespoons sugar
4½   teaspoons salt
3   tablespoons cider vinegar
1   cup raisins
¾   cup coarsely chopped walnuts
3   cups whole wheat flour
5   cups white flour (preferably unbleached)
3   tablespoons walnut oil (optional)
2   egg whites, slightly beaten

Crumble yeast into a large mixing bowl, add about 2 cups of warm water and let dissolve for about 5 minutes, or until yeast begins to bubble. Add sugar, salt, and vinegar and stir until dissolved. Stir in raisins, walnuts, and whole wheat flour. Stir in white flour, a cup at a time, until dough can be kneaded. Turn out onto a lightly floured surface and work in enough of remaining flour to form a smooth and elastic dough, kneading about 10 to 15 minutes.

Coat the inside of a large mixing bowl with walnut oil to flavor the dough and prevent it from sticking to the bowl as it rises. Place dough in the bowl and let it rise in a warm place until doubled in size, about 1½ to 2 hours. Punch dough down and let rise a second time, about 1 hour longer.

Preheat oven to 425 degrees.

Divide the dough into 2 or 3 parts, depending on the size of loaves preferred. Divide each part into 3 equal pieces and roll pieces between hands or on a lightly floured surface into long, tapered strands. Lay the three strands of dough side by side on the work surface and braid them loosely, starting from the center and working out toward each end. Finish by tucking ends under, twisting into a round knot or semicircle, or forming whatever shape you like.

Place loaves on buttered baking sheets, cover with a damp kitchen towel and let rise in a warm place for about 30 more minutes. Brush tops of loaves with the egg white, place in the middle of the oven and bake for 25 to 35 minutes or until their crusts are dark brown and loaves sound hollow when tapped on the underside.

Makes 2 to 3 loaves

Raisins and walnuts add taste and texture to whole wheat bread.

ROASTED SQUABS WITH CONCORD GRAPE AND LEEK SAUCE

8 squabs
4 cloves garlic, halved
4 tablespoons fresh thyme or 4 teaspoons dried
   Salt
   Freshly ground black pepper
¼ cup olive oil
½ cup butter, melted

SAUCE:
½ cup Armagnac
3 cups chicken stock
1 cup heavy cream
4 leeks, washed, trimmed, and cut into julienne strips
1½ pounds Concord or red grapes, halved and seeded

Preheat oven to 425 degrees.

Rub cavities of squabs with the cut side of garlic cloves and half the thyme and season with salt and pepper.

Drizzle oil and butter over the outside of each squab and sprinkle with remaining thyme. Place squabs on a rack in a roasting pan and bake for 15 minutes. Reduce oven heat to 350 degrees and continue cooking squabs for 15 to 20 minutes or until breasts are tender. Transfer squabs to a warmed serving platter and keep warm while preparing sauce.

Pour pan drippings into a saucepan. Deglaze roasting pan with the Armagnac and add to saucepan. Add stock and simmer over medium heat until reduced by one third. Stir in cream and reduce by one third again. Add leeks and grapes and simmer until warmed through.

Pour half the sauce over squabs and serve warm. Pass remaining sauce in a sauceboat.

Makes 8 servings

Note: For a picnic, squabs can be roasted as above, or grilled whole over hot coals for 25 minutes, and served without the sauce.

Overleaf: An antique American coverlet, French Quimper dinnerware, and grapevine baskets set the picnic buffet, which includes (left to right): scones filled with smoked turkey and gamay jelly, Roasted Squabs with Concord Grape and Leek Sauce, Corn Salad, Dorian Leigh Parker's Torta Rustica, and Vegetable Tian.

Colorful Torta Rustica features layers of poached salmon, eggs, cheese, and spinach.

DORIAN LEIGH PARKER'S TORTA RUSTICA

PASTRY DOUGH: (see note)

1	package active dry yeast
1	cup sweet butter, melted
6	eggs, beaten
4	cups flour
½	teaspoon salt

FILLING:

4	eggs
1	teaspoon fresh thyme, or ¼ teaspoon dried
2	pounds fresh spinach, steamed and chopped, or two 10-ounce packages frozen chopped spinach, thawed
½	cup whole milk ricotta cheese
¼	teaspoon freshly grated nutmeg
1	pound mozzarella cheese, thinly sliced
1	pound salmon, poached and flaked
2	tablespoons small capers

GLAZE:

1	egg
1	tablespoon heavy cream

Sprinkle yeast over ¼ cup lukewarm water in a small bowl and let dissolve. In a large mixing bowl, beat butter and eggs together. Stir in the yeast mixture, half the flour, and salt and blend well. Let mixture stand for 10 minutes, or until bubbles form.

Stir in remaining flour and blend well. Let dough stand, covered, in a warm place for about 1 hour, or until it has doubled in volume. Punch dough down, cover and refrigerate overnight, or for at least 6 hours. Remove from refrigerator 30 minutes before rolling out.

Preheat oven to 350 degrees.

Beat 4 eggs and thyme together in a small bowl until well blended. Pour half the eggs into a buttered and heated 7-inch crêpe pan or skillet and cook as you would an omelet until eggs are set. Flip omelet to cook other side briefly and turn out flat. Cook remaining half of eggs in the same manner, turn out and set aside.

In a large mixing bowl, combine spinach, ricotta, and nutmeg and set aside.

On a lightly floured work surface, roll out three fourths of the dough to a ½-inch thick round about 12 inches in diameter. Press dough into a springform pan 9 inches in diameter and 2 inches deep. The dough should come to top of pan.

Layer a third of the mozzarella slices on the bottom of the pastry shell. Top with one of the omelets, half the spinach-ricotta mixture, and half the salmon. Sprinkle with all of the capers, then repeat the layers, starting with another third of the mozzarella slices, the omelet, and all of remaining spinach and salmon. Top with remaining mozzarella.

Roll out remaining dough to a ½-inch thick round, slightly larger than 9 inches in diameter. Lay dough over the top of the torta, tucking edges inside to overlap slightly the sides of pastry shell. Cut a vent in top of dough to allow steam to escape.

Beat the egg and cream together in a small bowl and brush generously over the top of the dough. Bake in the center of the oven for 40 to 50 minutes, or until it is a rich golden brown. Let cool for 15 minutes before removing from the pan. Serve hot, warm, or at room temperature.

Makes 8 servings

Note: The dough should be made at least 6 hours before rolling it out.

Vegetable Tian served with plump yellow tomatoes.

VEGETABLE TIAN

1 pound fresh spinach leaves, or one 10-ounce package frozen chopped spinach, thawed
1 pound broccoli, cut into small flowerets
6 finger-size or 3 small zucchini, diced
1 tablespoon olive oil
2 medium onions, coarsely chopped
3 cloves garlic, crushed
½ cup fresh basil leaves, chopped, or 1 table-spoon dried
8 eggs
½ teaspoon freshly ground black pepper
   Salt
1 cup grated Parmesan cheese

Preheat oven to 350 degrees.

Using only the water remaining on leaves after rinsing, steam fresh spinach over high heat for about 4 minutes, or until wilted. Squeeze out excess water and chop. (If using frozen, squeeze all excess water out of thawed chopped spinach.)

In a large saucepan of lightly salted water, blanch broccoli for 2 or 3 minutes, or until it turns bright green. Drain. Blanch zucchini in same manner until crisp-tender. Drain. In a large skillet, heat olive oil, add onions and sauté over medium heat for 4 to 5 minutes, or until softened.

In a large mixing bowl, combine spinach, broccoli, zucchini, onions, garlic, and basil. In a separate bowl, beat the eggs and add pepper, add salt to taste, and ½ cup of the Parmesan.

Spoon vegetable mixture into a 1½-quart shallow baking dish. Pour the egg mixture over vegetables and top with remaining ½ cup cheese. Bake in the center of the oven for 20 to 25 minutes, or until eggs are set. Let cool to room temperature. Serve at room temperature.

Makes 6 servings

CONCORD GRAPE PIE

PASTRY DOUGH:

3	cups flour
1½	teaspoons sugar
½	teaspoon salt
1½	cups cold sweet butter, cut into pieces

FILLING:

3	pounds Concord grapes
1	cup sugar
⅓	cup cornstarch
	Freshly grated nutmeg (optional)

GLAZE:

1	egg
1	to 2 tablespoons heavy cream

In a large mixing bowl, combine flour, sugar, and salt. Add butter and cut into the dry ingredients with a fork or pastry blender until mixture resembles coarse meal. Toss in just enough cold water to make the dough stick together (3 to 5 tablespoons); do not overmix. Form into 2 flat cakes, wrap in plastic wrap, and chill for 15 to 30 minutes.

Working over a large bowl to catch juices, split grapes and remove pits with the tip of a sharp knife. Place grapes in a large sieve over the bowl and press them gently with the back of a spoon to extract ¾ cup of juice. Set grapes aside and reserve juice.

Preheat oven to 400 degrees.

In a medium saucepan, combine grape juice, sugar, and cornstarch. Bring to a boil and boil for 1 to 2 minutes, stirring constantly. Stir in the pitted grapes. Remove from the heat and let cool.

Roll out one part of pastry dough into a ⅛-inch thick round, 10 to 11 inches in diameter. Press dough gently into an 8- or 9-inch pie pan. Trim edges and crimp to make a decorative border. Turn the cooled filling into pie shell. If desired, sprinkle with freshly grated nutmeg.

Roll out remaining pastry dough to a round ⅛ inch thick and cut out several large grape-leaf-shaped pieces. Use the back of a sharp knife to outline veins on each leaf. Arrange leaves, stem ends toward the center, over the pie, overlapping them slightly so that the top of the pie is completely covered. Chill for 10 to 15 minutes.

Beat the egg and cream together well and brush over the top of the pie. Bake 15 minutes at 400 degrees. Reduce heat to 350 degrees and bake for about 40 minutes longer, or until the top is golden brown and the juices are bubbling.

Makes one 8- or 9-inch pie.

Fruit fresh from the vine and Concord Grape Pie.

A SURVIVOR'S MANUAL

THE AT-HOME
WEDDING

Mousse Tricolor with Dill Sauce

Cucumber Salad

Roast Loin of Herb Veal

Rosemary Potatoes

Haricots Verts

Lemon Sorbet

Ah the sweet seduction of the outdoor home wedding. Benign clouds floating across the sky, flowers nodding in tempo to the music of violins, and, strolling amid the gathering, a satisfied host, in the role of a latter-day Prospero, contemplates the successful magic.

A wedding is a unique occasion: unabashedly romantic, tinged with fantasy, and aimed toward an effect of seamless perfection that belies the weeks of careful preparation. Yet whether the event is to fete hundreds of guests or only a select few, many hosts prefer to take white tulle in hand and begin the serious business of planning a home reception.

For one young couple, Gene and Bonnie Pressman, the groom's parents' home in Harrison, New York, was the obvious choice for their early June wedding. Gently sloping lawns and pathways bordered with greenery and flowering shrubs offered a spacious outdoor setting for 250 guests and family to enjoy dining and dancing following the 6 o'clock wedding ceremony. With temperate weather and the clean, fresh air that is typical of the Long Island Sound, this outdoor wedding reception would set the formal aspects of ceremony and ritual against a landscape of casual, natural beauty.

To achieve this balance between traditional elegance and informality, the couple decided to have built a large (fifty-by-seventy-five foot) weatherproof tent. This billowy, diaphanous structure, placed in the garden, would permit the outdoor environment to pervade the scene with its charm of blossoming flowers and natural light, yet would also allow an interior area that could be designed and styled as desired. And in case of inclement weather, the tent would offer substantial protection so the party could continue without interruption.

A few days before the event, a crew of electricians and carpenters began construction work. After the tent was raised and secured with ropes and staves, a raised wooden platform was laid on the interior ground, then covered with industrial-strength carpet. Workers hung sparkling white lights and garlands of mountain laurel on the beams and walls, while cascades of balloons swayed from the rafters to contribute to the white-on-white fantasy.

Next a staff of professional decorators and their assistants began the elaborate task of setting each of the sixty-inch round tables. These were first covered with a backing of white foam rubber for bulk; cotton underliners were then smoothed on top; finally a layer of voile and of white moiré were added—the latter swagged in eight sections, each held in place by safety pins and tied with a triple bow of blue and white satin ribbons. Victorian fringed shades for the candles and an assortment of *objets* from the hostess's trove of collectibles—candy dishes, matchbook covers (replated in silver for the occasion), and ashtrays—added individuality to every table.

The wedding tent, within its garden setting.

Boldly colorful floral centerpieces, loosely arranged in antique country baskets, offered spectacular counterpoint to the white and silver color scheme of table linen and china. Natural garden flowers were used throughout, with clusters of hydrangea blossoms, pink climbing roses, daisies, Queen Anne's lace, and other flowers filling the tent with the fragrance and hue of a country field.

Expense is always a factor to be considered when entertaining, but an occasion as elaborate as a wedding requires a particularly detailed budget. Begin with a realistic total cost for the affair, then itemize the costs within each category: setting, flowers, music, decor, food, service. Advance planning allows a host time to think creatively within a financial limit. For example, table settings for the

For the reception, tables are covered with layers of voile and moire and swagged with satin ribbon. Candles with fringed shades, silver matchbook covers, and other collectibles are used as accents between centerpieces brimming with garden flowers.

Pressman wedding required 750 yards of fabric and 650 yards of satin ribbon; along with 25 floral arrangements for each of the tables at $250 each, the cost of these items alone would exceed the budget of many weddings. Less costly yet equally handsome alternatives might include the use of fewer fabrics per table, flower blooms instead of ribbons, and garden-grown flowers extended with sprays of baby's-breath for the centerpieces.

Of all aspects of the wedding celebration, the menu deserves particular attention. The food must be stimulating, appropriate to the hour of serving, convey a sense of festivity and celebration, yet also have general appeal. If it is to be served plated, waiters and serving help

Arrangements include roses, lilies, carnations, Queen Anne's lace, and hydrangea flowers.

Champagne and delicate tea sandwiches begin the festivities.

should be employed; if served buffet-style, advance preparation, flavor-retention, and texture-keeping qualities are important factors in determining menu choices.

Professional catering provided by Glorious Food of New York, including chefs, helpers, and fifty tuxedoed waiters ensures excellent service and imaginative dining for the wedding party and guests as they assemble in the tent for the reception. Delicate tea sandwiches, carefully garnished and arranged on trays, begin the meal after a Champagne toast to the newlywed couple. Served on assorted breads, the attractive canapés include egg salad, slices of ripe avocado liberally sprinkled with crisp bacon, cucumber, and watercress. For the first course, waiters present shimmering slices of Mousse Tricolor; a dark green layer of spinach is topped with a layer of delicate sole puréed with crème fraîche and heavy cream, and then a layer of fresh salmon similarly prepared. Slices of cucumber tossed with vinaigrette provide a cool, crisp accompaniment for the mousse, which is served with Chablis premier cru (1979).

As the Pressman party lingers over the first course, the caterers are hard at work in the kitchen of the nearby house completing last-minute work on the entrée. Roasted loin of veal, golden yet tender with a pink center, is cut into generous slices of moist, flavorful meat. Haricots verts, jade green and snappy fresh, and roasted potatoes, formed into perfect ovals and sprinkled with rosemary, accompany the veal. A well-rounded Château Lapelletrie (1978) is served with the main course.

Tender leaves of early summer endive and young bibb lettuce tossed with a light vinaigrette offer a refreshing salad course, and, appropriate to the formal tenor of the meal, an assortment of cheeses follows. For dessert the waiters present scoops of cool, tart lemon sorbet served in lemon shells, which clear sated palates for the grand finale—the traditional wedding cake. As it began, the meal so ended, with flutes of Moët et Chandon raised high to toast the bride and groom.

In order to attempt this ambitious menu without benefit of professional help, begin

A proper conclusion to the wedding meal—served with Champagne, of course.

with a detailed schedule of preparation, a careful calculation of the time necessary for advance as well as final cooking and preparation. Do as much shopping for ingredients as possible in advance, leaving only perishables to be purchased during the busy days just before the event. Helpers for cooking and serving are essential, so organize a crew that can assist both before and during the reception.

At one time or another, the voice of tradition beckons us all. Weddings are such occasions, when ritual and ceremony speak with a beauty and a pertinence that are ageless. And the home wedding, with its rare mixture of fantasy and familiar, epitomizes the affection and warmth that is at the heart of all memorable entertainments.

Mousse Tricolor served with Dill Sauce and Cucumber Salad.

MOUSSE TRICOLOR WITH DILL SAUCE

6	cups court bouillon (recipe follows)
2	tablespoons unflavored gelatin
1	pound fresh spinach leaves, stems removed
1	pound sole fillets, skinned
½	pound salmon fillets, skinned
6	slices black truffle (optional)
	Sprigs of fresh dill
1	teaspoon salt
½	teaspoon freshly ground white pepper
¼	teaspoon ground nutmeg
	Pinch cayenne pepper
¾	cup crème fraîche (see appendix) or sour cream
1	cup heavy cream, whipped
½	cup Béchamel sauce (see appendix)
2	cups dill sauce (recipe follows)

Place a 5-cup rectangular terrine or loaf pan in the refrigerator to chill.

In a medium saucepan, combine 3 cups of the court bouillon with the gelatin and heat slowly, stirring constantly, until gelatin has dissolved completely; do not let mixture boil. Set aside to cool and thicken slightly.

Drop spinach leaves into a large saucepan of lightly salted boiling water and blanch for about 5 minutes. Turn into a colander, rinse in cold water, and squeeze spinach dry in your hands, a small amount at a time.

Place the remaining 3 cups court bouillon in a large, straight-sided skillet and poach sole and salmon fillets separately, for about 4 minutes each. Drain fish and let cool. Discard poaching liquid or set aside for another use.

When aspic has thickened enough to coat the back of a spoon, pour into the chilled terrine, and rotate terrine until the entire inside surface is coated with aspic. Pour excess aspic back into saucepan and set aside. Refrigerate terrine until aspic is set. Repeat this process three times, heating aspic gently if it becomes too thick to pour, and reserving at least 6 tablespoons aspic for the mousses. Decorate bottom and sides of the aspic-lined terrine with truffles and/or dill sprigs and refrigerate until well chilled.

Combine salt, pepper, nutmeg, and cayenne in a small mixing bowl. Place the sole in a food processor with 2 tablespoons of the reserved aspic (warmed if necessary), and about a third of the seasoning mixture. Process until very smooth. Turn mixture into a mixing bowl and blend with ¼ cup crème fraîche. Fold in half the whipped cream. Spoon mixture into the bottom of the aspic-lined terrine, smoothing surface with a spatula, and chill.

Place salmon in the food processor with 2 tablespoons of the aspic and half of the remaining seasoning mixture, and process until very smooth. Turn into a mixing bowl and blend with remaining ½ cup crème fraîche. Fold in remaining whipped cream. Spoon mixture into terrine on top of sole mousse, smoothing surface with a spatula, and chill.

Prepare Béchamel sauce.

Place the spinach, Béchamel sauce, remaining 2 tablespoons of aspic, and remaining spice mixture in the food processor and process until very smooth. Spoon over the salmon mousse in the terrine, smoothing the surface with a spatula. Cover the top of the terrine with a sheet of waxed paper and chill for at least 8 hours.

To unmold, dip bottom and sides of the terrine in hot water for a few seconds and carefully invert onto a serving platter. Serve with dill sauce.

Makes 10 servings

Note: This mousse can be prepared a day in advance if desired.

Court Bouillon

2	sprigs parsley
1	bay leaf
2	sprigs thyme
1	stalk celery
1	carrot
1	onion, stuck with cloves
1	clove garlic
2	cups white wine
	Salt to taste
5	whole peppercorns

Tie together parsley, bay leaf, and thyme. Place in a large pot with remaining ingredients and 5 cups of water. Cover and bring to a boil. Simmer, uncovered, for 15 minutes. Strain and set aside until ready to use.

Dill Sauce

1	cup mayonnaise
½	cup crème fraîche (see appendix)
½	cup sour cream
2	tablespoons lemon juice
1	teaspoon dry white wine
	Salt and freshly ground black pepper to taste
	Pinch cayenne pepper
3	tablespoons chopped fresh dill

Combine all the ingredients and mix well. Refrigerate until ready to use.

Makes 2 cups

ROSEMARY POTATOES

10 Idaho potatoes
½ cup sweet butter, clarified (see appendix)
1 teaspoon chopped fresh rosemary leaves, or ½ teaspoon crushed dried
  Salt
  Freshly ground black pepper

Preheat oven to 400 degrees.

Peel potatoes and use a sharp paring knife to cut each into 2 ovals approximately 2½ inches long, making 20 pieces. Place them in a large shallow baking dish, pour clarified butter over and bake in the center of the oven for 15 minutes. Sprinkle potatoes with rosemary and return to the oven for 5 minutes more, or until tender. Sprinkle with salt and pepper to taste, toss lightly, and serve hot.

Makes 10 servings

ROAST LOIN OF HERB VEAL

1 3 to 3½-pound trimmed eye of veal loin with tenderloin
7 tablespoons butter, softened
1 teaspoon salt
¼ teaspoon freshly ground white pepper
1 tablespoon plus 1 teaspoon finely chopped shallots
½ teaspoon finely chopped basil
1 teaspoon finely chopped parsley
1 tablespoon olive oil
½ cup coarsely chopped onions
½ cup coarsely chopped carrots
½ cup coarsely chopped celery
2 cloves garlic, crushed
1 cup dry white wine
4 cups veal stock
½ cup dried morels, soaked overnight in 1 cup water, squeezed dry, soaking liquid reserved
1 cup heavy cream

Preheat oven to 400 degrees.

Set the tenderloin aside. Butterfly veal loin, splitting it lengthwise down the center without cutting all the way through. Spread the loin out, cut side up, on a flat surface and spread about 4 tablespoons of the softened butter evenly over the meat. Season with ½ teaspoon salt and ⅛ teaspoon pepper.

Melt 1 tablespoon of the remaining butter in a small skillet and sauté 1 teaspoon of the shallots over medium heat until softened. Combine sautéed shallots with basil and parsley on a piece of waxed paper and roll the tenderloin in herb mixture until well coated. Place the tenderloin in the center of the veal loin and sprinkle with any remaining herbs. Wrap the loin around the tenderloin and tie securely in several places with heavy string. Sprinkle with remaining salt and pepper, brush all over with olive oil and place in a roasting pan. Roast in the center of the oven for 15 minutes.

Reduce oven temperature to 350 degrees.

Combine onions, carrots, celery, and garlic, and place in the roasting pan around the roast. Continue to roast veal with the vegetables for 25 minutes longer.

Remove veal from the pan and keep it warm while preparing sauce. Add white wine to vegetables in roasting pan and warm on the stove over medium heat, stirring occasionally, for about 5 minutes. Add veal stock and reserved soaking liquid from morels and boil over high heat until reduced to about 2 cups, 15 to 20 minutes. Strain through a fine sieve.

In a medium saucepan, melt the remaining 2 tablespoons butter and sauté the remaining tablespoon of shallots until softened. Add morels and heavy cream, and simmer until thickened. Gradually add strained stock mixture, stirring constantly until smooth. Slice roast veal and serve immediately with the sauce.

Makes 10 servings

A handsome platter of Roast Loin of Herb Veal with Rosemary Potatoes and Haricots Verts.

CUCUMBER SALAD

6 medium cucumbers, peeled and cut in half
    lengthwise
1 teaspoon salt
1 cup vinaigrette (recipe follows)

Remove seeds from cucumbers with a teaspoon and cut into very thin slices. Place in a large mixing bowl and sprinkle with salt. Let stand for several hours.

Just before serving, pour off water and, pressing gently with the back of a wooden spoon, squeeze out excess liquid. Combine the cucumbers and vinaigrette in a serving bowl, toss thoroughly, and serve.

Makes 10 servings

Vinaigrette

¼ cup tarragon vinegar
 2 teaspoons Dijon-style mustard
    Salt to taste
¼ teaspoon freshly ground black pepper
⅔ cup olive oil

In a small mixing bowl, whisk together vinegar, mustard, salt, and pepper until well blended. Add oil in a slow, steady stream, whisking constantly, until blended.

Makes about 1 cup

HARICOTS VERTS

2   pounds haricots verts or young green
      beans, trimmed
1   tablespoon butter
2   shallots, finely diced
      Salt
      Freshly ground black pepper
2   tablespoons olive oil
2   tomatoes, peeled, seeded, and diced

Cook beans in a large saucepan filled with about 2 gallons of boiling salted water until crisp-tender, about 4 or 5 minutes. Rinse in cold water, drain, and let cool.

In a large skillet, melt butter over medium heat. Add shallots and sauté until softened. Add beans and sauté until warmed through. Season with salt and pepper to taste.

In another skillet, heat olive oil until very hot. Add diced tomatoes and sauté until excess liquid has evaporated.

Arrange beans on a serving platter and spoon tomatoes over them.

Makes 10 servings

LEMON SORBET

10   lemons
1½   cups sugar
1   egg white
10   sprigs fresh mint

Using a sharp paring knife, cut about 1 inch off the top or stem end of each lemon and about ¼ inch (or enough to allow lemon to stand firmly on a plate) off the opposite or bottom end. Grate rind from top and bottom pieces to produce 1 teaspoon of lemon zest; set zest and tops aside for decoration.

Being careful not to damage shells, cut the flesh away from the skin of each lemon and spoon flesh into a sieve. Place scooped-out lemon shells and the tops on a tray in the freezer. Extract the juice from the lemon pulp by pressing it through the sieve into a bowl. Set aside 1 cup lemon juice for the sorbet and reserve remaining juice for another use.

In a large, heavy saucepan, combine 3 cups cold water and sugar and bring to a boil over moderately high heat. Boil for 3 minutes; remove saucepan from heat and stir in lemon juice and reserved zest. Allow to cool. Meanwhile, in a small mixing bowl beat the egg white until soft peaks form.

Pour cooled lemon mixture into sorbet machine and freeze according to manufacturer's directions. Fold the egg white into the sorbet. Store in freezer until ready to serve. Spoon the sorbet into the frozen lemon shells just before serving, and decorate with mint leaves.

Makes 10 servings

Individual lemon shells filled with tart sorbet for dessert.

TWO FOR THE ROAD

PICNIC FOR LOVERS

TOAST POINTS WITH BELUGA CAVIAR AND
CREME FRAICHE

LENTIL SALAD

GRILLED BREAST OF SQUAB AND POUSSIN

YELLOW PEAR TOMATO
AND CUCUMBER SALAD

FRESH FRUIT AND CHEESE

There are landscapes that seem to be made for lovers: a rocky clearing in a remote woods in autumn; a small notch on the mountainside cosily accommodating a breakfast for two; or a little stretch of riverbank where lapping waves gleam in the light of a full moon at midnight. Whether the occasion is a planned celebration such as an intimate birthday or anniversary party, or a spontaneous picnic that just happens by itself on a gloriously mild day, nature provides lovers with a mood of privacy and stillness, raw materials for the sweet stuff of romance.

On this lazy Sunday morning, the late August sun touches California's Napa Valley with fat strokes of bronze light. Where a month ago heat rose in waves that made rippled seas of the acres of vineyards, now the landscape is calm and clear, with a fresh breeze blowing in lightly from San Francisco Bay. For one California couple, Jim and Sandy Connors, temperate weather and cloudless skies are all part of the master plan for the day; this is their tenth anniversary, and as celebration they have opted to pack picnic hampers and carryall bags with a collection of their favorite table linen, china, crystal, and silver, then drive to the Napa Valley for a languid, beautifully set picnic.

They have asked Cindy Pawlcyn, chef and co-owner of the Mustard Grille, a charming establishment nestled amid wineries in the town of Yountville, to create an elegant, portable feast. Accordingly, their first stop is at the restaurant, where the chef is waiting with baskets of food ready to be packed into the car. Cindy has responded to the couple's request for "food for romance" with a simple yet luxurious menu based on locally grown ingredients available in this fertile valley. "Living here is like being in heaven for a cook. You can get anything you want at a moment's notice by just calling up a local grower and asking for it," Cindy remarks, and points to baskets of fresh radicchio, tiny fingers of golden Finnish potatoes, and bunches of peppery mache greens. To enhance the fresh flavors and textures of this native produce, Cindy cooks in a clean, straightforward style based on simple preparations, fresh herbs, light sauces, and delicate marinades.

Since today's meal is for a special occasion, Cindy has added an extravagant touch to her simple—mostly native—approach. Beluga caviar and homemade crème fraîche on toasted slices of French baguette will be the first course along with a bottle of cold Champagne. For the entrée there are breasts of squab and poussin, the latter, a locally cultivated, sweet, young chicken. The poultry has been marinated in a mixture of garlic, orange juice, nutty sesame oil, and seasonings, then grilled until pink and juicy. Chilled and packed for the picnic, the poultry breasts will be dressed at serving time with a light citrus-flavored vinaigrette. For accompaniments to the main course there are yellow pear tomatoes, fresh

The elegantly presented lunch includes grilled poultry, yellow pear tomatoes and cucumbers, and fresh fruit and Stilton cheese.

cucumber wedges, and a lentil salad, robustly seasoned with garlic, red vinegar, scallion, and parsley.

At this time of year the Valley is at its prime in abundance, and the couple passes by acres of lush vineyards where emerald-bright leaves and healthy grapes intertwine in a dense profusion of growth. Adjacent gardens offer neat rows of crops, beefsteak and tiny, golden cherry tomatoes, Bibb and limestone lettuces, baby carrots, and summer squash.

Continuing in their leisurely pace, Jim and Sandy drive along narrow roads, undisturbed except by a few local residents out for a Sunday walk. In the shady courtyard behind a

Overleaf: An intimate picnic for two set in the Napa Valley.

An antipasto picnic includes crusty bread, hard salami, ripe olives, peppers, and red wine.

farmhouse, another picnic for two is underway. For this romantic pair, Frank and Meredith Waters, serene weather and the fact that it's Sunday are reasons enough to put together an impromptu luncheon. They begin by shopping for provisions at a nearby Italian market, one of many ethnic groceries in the Valley. In short order they assemble a variety of ingredients for an antipasto: spicy, hard salami, ripe olives covered with fresh herbs, homemade mozzarella cheese, and crusty rolls. The next stop is for a take-out pizza, freshly baked with ripe tomatoes, extra virgin olive oil, slivers of salty anchovy, and

There's no place like home—particularly when it's a backyard in the Napa Valley—for a luncheon of bubbly hot pizza and fresh summer fruit.